D1650446

The aim of the Biblical Classics Library is to make available at the lowest prices new editions of classic titles by well-known scholars. There is a particular emphasis on making these books affordable to Eastern Europe and the Two-Thirds World.

For current listing see overleaf

The Cruciality
of the Cross

The Cruciality of the Cross

P.T. Forsyth

paternoster
press

Copyright © 1997 Paternoster Press

First published in the UK 1909 by Independent Press Ltd.
Second Edition 1948
Third Impression 1955
Fourth Impression 1957

This edition published 1997 by
Paternoster Press in the Biblical Classics Library

03 02 01 00 99 98 97   7 6 5 4 3 2 1

Paternoster Press is an imprint of Paternoster Publishing,
P.O. Box 300, Carlisle, Cumbria CA3 0QS

British Library Cataloguing in Publication Data

A catalogue record for this book is available from the British Library.

ISBN 0-85364-835-2

Printed in Great Britain by Mackays of Chatham PLC, Kent

CONTENTS

I

PAGE

THE ATONEMENT CENTRAL TO THE NEW TESTAMENT
GOSPEL. 11

II

THE ATONEMENT CENTRAL TO CHRISTIAN EXPERIENCE 40

III

THE ATONEMENT CENTRAL TO THE LEADING FEATURES
OF MODERN THOUGHT 55

IV

THE MORAL MEANING OF THE BLOOD OF CHRIST . 58

NOTE

THE first two chapters of this book were given in substance as the opening address of the Third International Congregational Council at Edinburgh in July 1908.

The third was really an undelivered section of the first, and it appeared in the *Hibbert Journal* for April 1909. It is here by the kind permission of the Editor.

And the fourth appeared in an unfinished form in the *Expositor* for September 1908.

All are much revised, amended and expanded.

PREFACE

FORGIVENESS THROUGH ATONEMENT THE ESSENTIAL OF EVANGELICAL CHRISTIANITY

I. In respect of the New Testament
II. In respect of Christian Experience
III. In respect of Modern Thought

ONE of the acutest problems of the Church at this moment is that raised by the pressure of the critical method upon the New Testament. It is not only how to apply to the New Testament the criticism which has been so fruitful with the Old Testament. That is intricate enough, and much more intricate for the New Testament than for the Old Testament. But the problem is more than intricate. It is profound and spiritual. It comes nearer than Old Testament problems do to the centre of the soul, the word of conscience, the essence of faith, and our eternal hope. It makes a call upon the personality more than the ability. Its conclusions make a confession of faith and not a statement of view. We have to apply criticism to the New Testament, regardful of the fact that we have there what we do not have in the Old Testament. We have everything clustering round a historic personality with whom the soul is in direct and living communion to-day, everything gathered round a final and eternal act of God as the consummation of that personality—an act which fundamentally altered the whole moral relation of the race to Him. We have to do in the New Testament with the person of Christ and with the cross of Christ. And in the last issue with the cross of Christ, because it is the one key to His person.

In approaching this subject let us be clear about our starting-point. It is the Church and its moral faith. The truth of Christianity cannot be proved to the man in the street till he come off the street by owning its power. In our modern psychology we start from the primacy of the will, and we bring everything to the test of man's practical and ethical life. And so, here also we start ethically from the holiness of God as the supreme interest in the Christian revelation. The standpoint taken by the Church is that which I believe to be the position of the New Testament. That book represents a grand holiness movement; but it is one which is more concerned with God's holiness than ours, and lets ours grow of itself by dwelling on His. Christianity is concerned with God's holiness before all else; which issues to man as love, acts upon sin as grace, and exercises grace through judgment. The idea of God's holiness is inseparable from the idea of judgment as the mode by which grace goes into action. And by judgment is meant not merely the self-judgment which holy grace and love stir in man, but the acceptance by Christ of God's judgment on man's behalf and its conversion in him to our blessing by faith.

By the atonement, therefore, is meant that action of Christ's death which has a prime regard to God's holiness, has it for its first charge, and finds man's reconciliation impossible except as that holiness is divinely satisfied once for all on the cross. Such an atonement is the key to the incarnation. We must take that view of Christ which does most justice to the holiness of God. This starting-point of the supreme holiness of God's love, rather than its pity, sympathy, or affection, is the watershed between the Gospel and the theological liberalism which makes religion no more than the crown of humanity and the metropolitan province of the world. My point of departure is that Christ's first concern and revelation was not simply the forgiving love of God, but the holiness of such love.

So viewed the atonement is central—

I. To the New Testament Gospel;

II. To Christian experience;

III. To the leading features of modern thought.

And by centrality is meant something far more than that the doctrine is the pivot of an adjusted and balanced system of thought, something much more vital and effective for moral life and the life of the soul. By centrality is meant finality for human history and destiny. It is meant that when Jesus died for our sins He died once for all, that He did not merely signalise in a classic way the expiation all must dree, and illustrate and cheer every man's atonement for his own misdeeds. It is meant beyond that, first, that in the atonement we have primarily the act of God, and the act of God's holiness; second, that it alone makes any repentance or expiation of ours satisfactory to God; and third, that as regards man it is a revolutionary act, and not merely a stage in his evolution. It is further meant that our view of what Christ was and did must be the view that does most justice to the holiness of God and takes most profoundly and seriously the hallowing of His name.

A true grasp of the atonement not only meets many positive features of the present age, but above all it meets the age in its need and impotence, its need of a centre, of an authority, of a creative source, a guiding line, and a final goal. It goes with our best positive tendencies, and it meets our negative need, our lack of a fixed point. All around us is in a growing flux; change is everywhere; and it may or may not be development according as our fixed standard and goal may be. With no centre, either for its own action or for our estimate, it means disintegration. And especially does our religion need a moral centre. It grows on the one hand evolutionary, and therefore inevitably unearnest; and on the other hand sentimental. It harps on love till it reaches the condition of those decently demoralised people who read nothing but the literature of love, dwell on nothing else, slacken every moral fibre by the submission to this of every other interest in life, and finally gravitate to a chief interest in its morbid or immoral forms. Fraternity grows at the cost of fidelity, the democratic sympathies and pities monopolise the moral world, the moral type changes, and another scale of virtues fills the ideal. "Among the working class," says Miss Loane from a long experience as district nurse, "generosity ranks before justice, sympathy before truth, love before chastity, a pliant and obliging disposition before a rigidly honest one. In brief," she continues, "the less admixture of intellect required for the practice of any virtue the higher it stands in the popular estimation." But what does that mean but the retreat of the protestant type of life before the Roman, of the evangelical virtues before the catholic, of heroic faith before humanist, of Paul before Pelagius? It means the removal of authority from a positive centre in Christ's redeeming act to what I might call a diffused centre in the heart, from a new moral man once for all in the cross to the man periodically renewed in kindly sacraments. What is lacking to current and weak religion is the very element supplied in the atoning cross as the reconciling judgment of the world.

That is the general theme which I would enlarge.

I

THE CENTRALITY OF THE ATONEMENT
TO THE NEW TESTAMENT GOSPEL

IN regard to Christ's cross, and within the New Testament,
we are to-day face to face with a new situation. We are
called upon, sometimes in the tones of a religious war, to
set Jesus against Paul and to choose between the historic
and the biblical Christ. We are bidden to release Jesus from
Paul's arrest, to raise Him from that tomb in which He was
buried by the apostle of the resurrection, and to loose Him
and let Him go. The issue comes to a crisis in the interpretation of the death of Christ. To treat that death as more
than a martyrdom, or to allow it more than a supreme
degree of the moral effect upon us of all self-sacrifice, is
called a gratuitous piece of theology. To treat it as anything
more than the seal of Jesus's own faith in the love of God,
or in His prophetic message of reconciliation, is to sophisticate. To regard it as more than the closing incident in a life
whose chief value lies in its history (which all the time
criticism slowly dissolves), is a piece of perverse religious
ingenuity much more like the doctrine of Transubstantiation.
To regard it as having anything to do with God's judgment
on man's sin, or as being the ground of forgiveness, is a
piece of grim Judaism or gloomy Paulinism. The death of
Jesus had no more to do with sin than the life of Jesus; and
Jesus in His life made no such fuss about sin as Christianity
has done. The death of Jesus had really no more to do with
the conditions of forgiveness than any martyr's. Every man
must make his own atonement; and Jesus did the same, only
on a scale corresponding to the undeniable greatness of
His personality, and impressive accordingly.

Such teaching removes Christ from the Godhead of
grace and makes Him but a chief means of grace to fellow-
seekers. But a Church of the Gospel is not a band of disciples

or inquirers, but a community of believers, confessors, and regenerates in Christ's cross. An evangelical Church has stood, and stands, not only for the supreme value of Christ's death, but for its prime value as atonement to a holy God, and as the only atonement whereby man is just with God. The atonement which raises that death above the greatest martyrdom, or the greatest witness of God's love, is for us no piece of Paulinism.

Of course, we have all felt the reticence of the Gospels on that doctrine. But how can we avoid feeling its real presence in them except by coming to them with a dogmatic humanism, or a heckling criticism, or a conscience mainly æsthetic? Why, the most advanced New Testament criticism is now concerned to show that the main interest of the evangelists is not biographical, but dogmatic on such matters as baptism and atonement and the last things. The Gospels stand at least on the atoning deed, they were written for a Church which was created by it, and they give singular space to it. Even in John, Jesus is not a disguised God urging people to pierce His veil; He is there to do a work that only His death could do, as a corn of wheat must die to bear. And the Epistles are full of the meaning of that deed.

And where did their interpretation of its meaning come from? From Paul's rabbinism? From the Judaism of his upbringing? From the fanciful speculations of his environment? Was it an interpretation or an importation? Well, where does Paul himself say he got the atoning conception of Christ's death? He received it from the Lord? What does that mean? Was it really but some flash of insight peculiar to his own genius or his idiosyncracy? Was it a feat of ingenious interpretation? No doubt it took, in certain lights, the colour of his rabbinic mind; but was it in essence just an original and daring application of Judaic theology to the crucifixion? Was it a brilliant construction, a re-orientation of his traditional theology, whose flash he mistook for a special revelation? No, in its substance it was a part of the

Christian instruction which completed his conversion at Damascus. It was from his teachers that he had the atoning interpretation of Christ's death. He delivered to his Churches what he received among the fundamentals ($\dot{\epsilon}\nu$ $\pi\rho\dot{\omega}\tau o\iota\varsigma$) from earlier Christians (1 Cor. xv. 3, xi. 23), that Christ died for our sins, that His blood was shed for their remission, that His death set up a new relation or covenant between God and man, and that all Israel's history and Bible meant this. In the year 57, that is, he states that such was the common faith of the apostolic community when he was converted, three or four years after Christ's death. It was nothing he developed or edited, but it was something which came from Jesus Himself. Paul received it from the Lord because it came to him from those who had so received it at first.

And how came the apostolic circle to have this view of Christ's death? Could *they* have foisted on the cross an interpretation so audacious? Must they not have been taught by Christ so as to view it in such forms as are echoed in the ransom passage and at the Last Supper? Must they not have been taught, then, by Christ either during the forty days or from within the veil? They declare they were taught many new things by Him from heaven. We have the same idea, with natural enough variants, in Peter, in John, and in Hebrews. No; the first teacher of the atonement was the Christ who made it. It is no Paulinism, except in certain side lights. Had the apostles held the humanist view that what mattered was but the life, character and teaching of Christ, would they have given the hand of fellowship to Paul when he came to them with the view that biography mattered little compared with Christ's death? Would Paul have taken their hand, with that gulf between them? And what a gulf! It is at bottom all the gulf between the genial Judaism of Hillel which let Christ go to His death as a fanatic and the Christianity which found in His death His deity. The whole history of the Church shows that there can be no standing unity of faith, spirit, or fellowship between those to whom Christ's death is but a great martyrdom and those to whom it is the one atonement of the world and God, the one final treatment of sin, the one compendious work of grace, and the one hinge of human destiny.

We have been warned against the idea that Christ taught about Himself or His work as an essential element of His own Gospel. We are told that He is detachable from His Gospel, if not in history yet in principle. We received it through Him, to be sure, but we do not necessarily have it in Him. But let us leave the question whether He taught Himself, and go back to the prior question. Does the Gospel, does Christianity consist primarily of what Jesus taught? Is that the whole Gospel? Is it the focus of it? Or the standard? Is the Gospel confined to the Galilean ministry? Are we to test every teaching of an apostle by what is left us of the teaching of the Master—either by that alone or by that in chief? Where in the New Testament do we find the authority for that limitation? Where does Jesus impose it? It is surely clear that those He taught never understood Him so. If they had, could they have done anything else than go about retailing that teaching, with a lament at its premature arrest? But is that what they did? The prime thing, and the earliest thing, we know about their teaching (I have just said) is that Christ crowned Israel by dying for the world's sins. It has not the note of regret, nor has it the note of transmitted precept. When precepts were wanted they made new ones for the occasion, on the free evangelical principle, and not on the canonist. They applied the redemption to particular junctures freely, in the spirit; they did not make a casuistic application of Christ's maxims. They did not attack Jew or Gentile even with the parables. James himself, who might have been expected to abjure the Pauline method, and take the strictly ethical line, does not draw his precepts from the armoury of synoptic injunction, or treat Christ as the Chief Rabbi of Israel. Nay, they did not even work with the mere personal impression made on them by Jesus, with the magnetism of a personality whose acts or whose words another Rabbi might criticise. They worked with His person as itself the message, and the final message. They worked with a faith which was not a piece of impressionism but the worship of their new creator, and which therefore did not fade as an impression does, but grew as a new life. Whether Christ taught Himself or not, what He gave, what He left behind, was Himself above all; and Himself as no mere impressionist but as the Saviour, the New Creator. His legacy was neither a truth nor a collection of them, nor a character and its imaginative memory, but a faith that could not stop short of giving Him the worship reserved by all the past for God alone. And what caused this? What produced this result, so amazing, so blasphemous for Jews? It was the cross, when it came home by the resurrection through the Spirit. It was then that Jesus became the matter and not merely the master of gospel preaching. It was then that He became Christ indeed, then when He became perfected! Perfected! He became the finished Saviour only in the finished salvation. And, for those who worshipped Him first, all He was to them centred in the cross and radiated from there. It was the Christ who was made sin for them in the cross that became for them God reconciling the world to Himself. He was all to them in the cross, where He died for their sin, and took away the guilt of the world, according to their Scriptures. It was then that He finished the universal task latent in their national religion, and dealt once for all before God with the sin of the world. That was the starting-point of the Gospel, that made it missionary, made the Church. It is the content of the Gospel. And it is always to there that the Church must come back, to take its bearings, and be given its course.

The very silence of Christ makes His atonement the holiest place of Christian faith. But it was not absolute silence. It was reserve. And He broke it in Paul. The exposition in the Epistles is the Saviour's own work upon His work. He becomes His own divine scholiast. If He lived in Paul submerging Paul (Gal. ii. 20) then Paul's word here was a continuation of Christ's work. It is Christ, the Lord the Spirit, giving that account of Himself which in the Gospels was restrained, partly for want of an audience that could understand or a disciple that could apprehend. His earthly silence is not so surprising. If He showed Himself after His resurrection only to the disciples, if He refused to make it a miraculous appeal to the sceptical world, so, in the still holier matter of His cross, He may well have been reserved, even to His own. The great doers are greatly dumb. And Christ was straitened in the doing of the mighty work. But His Church—it is no wonder that His Church has been prompt to praise it, keen to pierce it, and eager to construe it. For the Church is the organ which cannot but speak and praise when the Master's silent touch on the keys sets free its soul.

It is sometimes said that the great question of the hour for the Church's belief is Christological; it is the question of Christ's person. That is true. But it is the question of the cross all the same. We know the Incarnation only as the foundation of the cross. It is from the base of His cross that the stair descends to it. For the question of the Christ is the question of the Saviour. It is not a metaphysical question, but a religious. It is not philosophical, but experimental. It is theological chiefly as being ethical—as turning on sinful man's practical relation to the ethic of eternity, which is the conscience of a Holy God. The question of Christ is not the question of a divine hypostasis, but of a divine Saviour. Technically spoken, the Christology turns on a Soterology.

But the question of a Saviour is the question of a salvation. It turns on an experience, and not only on an experience, and the experience of a historic person, but upon what is for us a *revolutionary* experience, and not a mere impression, however deep. It turns on a new creation. The sot*ero*logy turns on a soter*io*logy. The centre of Christ is where the centre of our salvation is. He is Christ, He is God, to us in that He saves us. And He is God by that in Him which saves us. He is Christ and Lord by His cross. Christian faith is our life-experience of complete forgiveness and final redemption in Christ. It does not *include* forgiveness; it *is* forgiveness. Its centre is the centre of forgiveness. Only the redeemed Church, the Church that knows the forgiveness, has the key to the Saviour. His blessings are the key to His nature; they do not wait till the nature is first defined. No philosopher, as such, has the key, no theologian, no scholar, no critic; only the believer, only the true Church. And we have it where the evangelical experience has always found its forgiveness—in the cross. Our faith begins with the historic Christ. But not with the biography of Christ (except for propædeutic purposes). We begin, in principle if not in method, with Christ the crucified. We begin with the Church's saving faith in Christ, and not with the modern man's fair verdict on Him. We do not begin with a writer's picture of Christ the prophet, but with the work of Christ the Saviour, continuous in the Church that it made, and made the mother of our own soul. Mere historic knowledge can create no salvation which is not given by certainty about a historic fact, nor by any intelligent grasp of it, but by faith in it, by faith in that within it which is super-historic. And faith finds in this fact of the cross worlds more than a prophet's martyrdom. It finds the depth of God in action, and not merely the depth of the martyr's convictions. The Christ that we trust all to is not one who died to witness for God, but one in whom God died for His own witness, and His own work on us. God was in Christ reconciling. The prime doer in Christ's cross was God. Christ was God reconciling. He was God doing the very best for man, and not man doing his very best before God. The former is evangelical Christianity, the latter is humanist Christianity. Christ's history, His person, can only be understood by His work, and by a work that we apprehend in our moral experience even when we cannot comprehend it by our intelligence. We believe with the unity of our person much that we cannot yet reduce to logical unity. And our soul, our self, finds itself in Him long before our mind does—just as, in the case of His own life, He but gradually appropriated and realised by experience the content of His own personality. The Christ we worship is Christ as forgiver, as redeemer, as new creator, and as judge of all. His relation to the God of thought is something we can wait for; it is a question of the metaphysic, or the theosophy, of Christian faith and ethic. Personal faith may overleap the centuries and go straight to the Bible Christ. But reason with any belief in evolution cannot do so. The science, the theology, of faith cannot do so. It is bound to develop the creed of the Church and not to discard it like some novelist turned theologian without capital. It is bound to correct and adjust as it develops the creed. To turn it out of doors and start on one's own account on nothing is intellectual pertness. And the Church's belief in the divinity of Christ is the result of her experience of justifying faith, of being restored and raised into the communion of God by union with His Christ in faith. To be united with Christ is, in our experience, to be united with God. Therefore, Christ is God. I am redeemed in Christ, and only God can redeem.

Our chief natural legacy from the past is distance and alienation from God. The chief problem of the present (and of every present) is to reduce and destroy that. It is reconciliation. But reconciliation is no æsthetic, or educational, or impressionist affair. It is not a revival. It is not a question of touching a certain number of individuals, and gathering them for salvation out of a lost mankind. It cannot be done by a magnetic temperament, a noble character, or a lofty sage. It means changing a whole race's relation to God. For good and all that could only be done from God's side; and it was done in the cross. We have to be redeemed into that reconciliation, and redeemed as a race. It was a work that had to be done, and not merely a personal influence that was to be conveyed. Christ did not die simply to affect men but to effect salvation, not simply to move man's heart but to accomplish God's will. All we may do to reconcile men to God is but the following up of a great and final deed of God—the cross.

It is the cross, then, that is the key to Christ. None but a Christ essentially divine could do what the Church beyond all other knowledge knows the cross to have done for its soul. The divinity of Christ is what the Church was driven upon to explain the effect on it of the cross. Nothing less could explain the new creation, which is so much deeper than any impression on us, and calls for an author so much more than prophetic, hortatory, or impressionist in soul. The atonement of the cross is the key that opens the door, but the house we enter is not made with hands. It is the very heart of God we have in Christ. We are not landed in a vestibule but straight in the sanctuary of the place. This Son of God is God the Son.

II

In the life of Dr. Dale it is mentioned that in his closing years he was much impressed with the remark of a friend that it was high time the word grace returned to our preaching. He felt that it had been ousted by the word love, in our vehement reaction from theological orthodoxy. And he knew that any gospel of love which was not dominated by the idea of grace had but a short and feckless life before it.

Now, though the idea of grace has returned to our preaching, it has not returned to an extent that would have satisfied Dr. Dale. And one reason for that is that the attention of the Christian public in the interval has been deflected. It has been deflected towards social sympathies, at the cost of personal, experimental, and I will say ethical religion. At the cost of ethical religion, I will say. For we have lost the sense of sin, which is the central issue of all ethic because it turns on the relation of the conscience to the conscience of God. And apart from sin grace has little meaning. The decay of the sense of sin measures our loss of that central Christian idea; and it is a loss which has only to go on to extinguish Christianity.

It is reported from most quarters in England that there is a serious decline in Church membership. For this several explanations are given. But it is well to face the situation, and to avoid extenuation. And if we do, we may discover that the real cause is the decay, not in religious interests or sympathies, but in personal religion of a positive and experienced kind, and often in the pulpit. Religious sympathies or energies are not Christian faith. Faith is Christian certainty. We have become familiar with the statement (so welcome to easy religion) that there is as good Christianity outside the Churches as in. This is not quite false, but it is much more false than true. It would be true enough if Christianity meant decent living, nice ways, precious kindness, business honour, ardent philanthropy, and public righteousness. But all these fine and worthy things are quite compatible with the absence of personal communion with God, personal faith as Christ claims it, in the sense of personal experience of God in Jesus Christ, personal repentance, and personal peace in Christ as our eternal life. Yet that is God's first charge on us if Christianity be true. And it is the kind of Christianity which alone makes for a Church and its membership. A Christianity merely ethical, refined, or sympathetic certainly makes for the social state, if you can keep it up; but the Christianity that makes for the Church is of a much more intimate, personal, and positive kind. And its presence is the only guarantee for the maintenance of the moral strength and beauty of society at the last. While its absence must not only diminish the roll of membership but reduce interest in the great religious issue between Church and State. The reports that come in are as clear about the cooling of that interest as they are about the drop in the membership of the Churches. The decay in membership of the Church is due to a decay of membership in Christ. Our social preoccupation has entailed real damage to personal and family religion. For even among those who remain in active membership of our Churches the type of religion has changed. The sense of sin can hardly be appealed to by the preacher now, and to preach grace is in many (even orthodox) quarters regarded as theological obsession, and the wrong language for the hour, while justification by faith is practically obsolete. Well, it may be wise not to preach too often about grace, though we cannot preach too much (indeed, what have we at last but grace to preach?); but it is fatal if our reserve is because we do not have it, instead of because we reverence it, if the reason be defect of truth and not its economy.

I know what is said in reply, and it is said with much force. It is said that the sense of sin has not departed but has only changed its form. We are more dull to individual sin because we are more alive to social sin. We have public compunction instead of personal repentance.

To that remark I would answer two things.

First. Public compunction does not move to seek forgiveness, which is the prime righteousness of the Kingdom of God, but to pursue redress and reform. And redress and reform is not what makes Christianity. Christianity is a religion of redemption, but that is a religion of amelioration or assuagement. It is engrossed with the wrong done to our brother and not to our God, and it is therefore to that extent the less religious.

But second. The tendency is welcome in so far as this, that we cannot stop there. The more public we make the sin, the more social and racial, so much the more are we driven upon a treatment of it which is ethical and not temperamental, which is racial as well as personal, and not only racial but divine. Now there is no treatment of it which satisfies these demands of the soul, the conscience, society, and God, but the atonement in Christ's cross. In the old juridical theories the social, or racial, aspect of the atonement, its connection with the moral order, is one of the great truths. And the more these theories become unsatisfactory on other grounds the more should the truth of their social sense of sin be developed in terms of modern society. But then the more sin is socialised so much the more imperative becomes the necessity of an atonement. As man grows the sin grows. The kingdom of evil grows with the kingdom of good. Sin, self, exploits every stage in the progress of society. It becomes unified, organised, and it must therefore be dealt with at a centre. The social organism has a common and organic sin. And a collective sin must have a central treatment. The more I lament and amend social wrongs the more I must realise before God the responsibility for them of me and mine. It is not only the plutocrats. If it is man that is wronged it is man that has wronged him, it is man that has sinned, man that is condemned. You cannot split up the race. You insist, indeed, on its solidarity. Its unity and solidarity is one of the commonplaces of modern thought. Surely, therefore, if sin there be, man is the sinner. The wrong inflicted on man sets up a corresponding responsibility on man at his centre. There must be a central and solidary treatment of sin and one where responsibility is borne in man, even though it be vicariously. And any atonement becomes a matter of judgment, and not mere repentance or reparation. That seems inevitable if we believe in responsibility, and also believe in the unity of the human race. It seems logical.

But there is much more than logic in it. It comes home far more mightily and solemnly from the belief in another unity, the belief in the absolute moral unity of God, in a word, a real belief and a real sense of His holiness.

To bring sin home, and to bring grace home, we need that something else should come home which alone gives meaning to both—the holy. The grace of God cannot return to our preaching or to our faith till we recover what has almost clean gone from our general, familiar, and current religion, what liberalism has quite lost—I mean a due sense of the holiness of God. This sense has much gone from our public worship, with its frequent irreverence;

from our sentimental piety, to which an ethical piety with its implicates is simply obscure; from our rational religion, which banishes the idea of God's wrath; from our public morals, to which the invasion of property is more dreadful than the damnation of men. If our Gospel be obscure it is obscure to them in whom the slack God of the period has blinded their minds, or a genial God unbraced them, and hidden the Holy One who inhabits eternity. This holiness of God is the real foundation of religion—it is certainly the ruling interest of the Christian religion. In front of all our prayer or work stands "Hallowed be Thy name." If we take the Lord's Prayer alone, God's holiness is the interest which all the rest of it serves. Neither love, grace, faith, nor sin have any but a passing meaning except as they rest on the holiness of God, except as they arise from it, and return to it, except as they satisfy it, show it forth, set it up, and secure it everywhere and for ever. Love is but its outgoing; sin is but its defiance; grace is but its action on sin; the cross is but its victory; faith is but its worship. The preacher preaches to the divinest purpose only when his lips are touched with the red coal from the altar of the thrice holy in the innermost place. We must rise beyond social righteousness and universal justice to the holiness of an infinite God. What we on earth call righteousness among men, the saints in heaven call holiness in Him.

Have our Churches lost that seal? Are we producing reform, social or theological, faster than we are producing faith? Have we become more liberal than sure? Then we are putting all our religious capital into the extension of our business, and carrying nothing to reserve or insurance. We are mortgaging and starving the future. We are not seeking first the Kingdom of God and His holiness, but only carrying on, with very expansive and noisy machinery, a "kingdom-of-God-industry". We are merely running the kingdom; and we are running it without the cross—with the cross perhaps on our sign, but not in our centre. We have the old trade mark, but what does that matter in a dry and thirsty land where no water is, if the artesian well on our premises is going dry?

To bring *sin* home, and *grace* home, then, the *Holy* must be brought home. But that again can be done, on the scale of the Church and the world, only by replacing the *cross* at the centre of Christian faith and life, as an atonement not indeed to outraged dignity, nor to talionic justice, but to this holy love. The centrality of the cross belongs to it only as a holy and atoning cross. Only if Christ atoned for the world did he culminate in the cross, and do the great thing there. And it is as an atonement that the Church has kept the cross at its spiritual centre. This is still the moral problem of the Church in relation to society, to keep the gospel of the cross at the centre. The form, indeed, of the Church's moral problem will always depend on the social conditions of the hour; but the substance of it is always the same. It is practical. It is to place the moral centre of society upon the moral centre of the soul, upon the centre of the moral universe. And what is that but to place the conscience of society on Calvary? What is our task to-day? It is to take the mass of men (and not only the masses)—inert and hopeless some, others indifferent, others hostile to God—and to reconcile them with God's holy will and righteous kingdom; but to reconcile them less with the *ideal* of a kingdom of God than with His *way* of it. They are keen enough about a kingdom which glorifies human ideals, but the trouble is about God's ideal and God's way, about Christ and His cross as the way as well as the goal. The task is to destroy our national and social dislike of that enthusiasm of the cross, to supplant lust by that higher ardour, to bend the strongest wills to the obedience of the holiest, and by moral regeneration to restore men both physically and socially. This is a tremendous task. It is the whole object of history. It is far beyond socialism. And no laws can do it, and no change of circumstances, but only Jesus Christ. It is the fruit of His work, of His holy love,

His holy spirit, and His holy Church, all flowing from His holy cross. Let us not mistake the kindly fruits of the cross for the moral principle of it. The fruits will not give the principle, but the principle will give the fruits. And the more we are preoccupied with social righteousness so much the more we are driven to that centre where the whole righteousness of God and man found consummation, and adjustment, and a power and a career, in the saving judgment of Christ's cross. Public liberty rest on inward freedom; and the cross alone gives moral freedom, and moral independence, to the mass of men, who were left to slavery even by the heroic moral aristocracy of stoicism. It is the cross that makes moral worth an infectious power, keeps character from being self-contained, and gives a moral guarantee of a steady social future. The cross is the spring, not of self-possessed and individualist righteousness, but of that creative and contagious goodness which makes possible the social state. Only at the centre of the cross does the man find himself in his kind, and both in God. A creative, missionary, and social ethic springs only from religion; and it springs most from the religion which is able to clothe us with the power of the creative, loving, outgoing God.

III

When we speak of the centrality of the Atonement, I have said, we mean much more, worlds more, than its place in a religious system. We are speaking of that which is the centre, not of thought, but of actual life, conscience, history and destiny. We speak of what is the life-power of the moral world and its historic crisis, the ground of the Church's existence, and the sole meaning of Christ Himself. Christ is to us just what His cross is. All that Christ was in heaven or on earth was put into what He did there. And all that man's moral soul needs doing for it eternally was done centrally there. Neither cross nor Christ is simply a historic fact by which we order our mental calendar; they make the sun in our heaven, the force in our world. They make our vital centre, not as mere facts, but as sacraments; not for their occurrence, but for their significance; not because we reckon from them, but because we live from them.

It is sometimes said, "There are several theories of the Atonement, but we have to do with the fact, and not with our understanding of it." This frame of mind is the root of all that is most feeble and ominous in our Churches to-day. The one thing we need is to understand the Atonement, with a life's understanding, with a vital conscience. There it is that Christ comes to Himself for good. There, as it were, He finally finds His tongue, and takes command of the deep eloquence of moral things. Christ, I repeat, is to us just what His cross is. You do not understand Christ till you understand His cross. Nor have you measured the moral world. Such a fact as Christ or His Atonement only exists as it is intelligible, as it comes home to us with a moral meaning and a moral nature. It is only by understanding it that it becomes anything else than a martyrdom, that it becomes the saving act of God. It is only by understanding it that we escape from religion with no mind, and from religion which is all mind, from pietism with its lack of critical judgment, and from rationalism with its lack of everything else.

If I may be pardoned for another reference to Dr. Dale, he said that one of our great needs was more preaching about Christian ethics. Well, since his time that need has been largely met, especially in the religion of social ethics. Perhaps, indeed, it has been overdone, considering the amount of insight into ethical principle which we mostly have at command. We have been made to attend to the Christian life, in the sense of Christian conduct, at the expense of the Christian life in the inner sense of justifying faith. Ethic has been externalised. The effect of faith in conduct has been ethicised, but the nature of faith in experience has not; it has been sentimentalised. The centre of gravity has been transferred from the cross to the parable of the prodigal. So that what we need is the ethicising of religion itself, and not simply of the fruits of religion. We want a religion ethical in itself, in its nature, genius and effect; we want more than a manner of life which is morality suffused with piety. And to ethicise religion there must be restored to it, from its centre, that note of judgment which it has lost, that note of supreme reference to a holy God. The moralising of Christian conduct is not the moralising of Christian faith. Yet it is the faith that needs moralising most. If conduct is wrong, it is the religion that needs reforming; the life will follow the faith. And to reform our religion we must be driven, not only *to* its centre but *into* its centre. You seek the ethicising of religion, its rescue from theology and sentiment? Well, you can only get it by theology. The prime need of religion to-day is a theology. No religion can survive which does not know where it is. And current religion does not know where it is, and it hates to be made to ask. It hates theology.

The ethicising principle of religion must be the creative element at its source. Has it a moral source? To answer that question is theology; and it is a theology of judgment. Ours is an eternal faith, and it can only be moralised by the eternal righteousness, *i.e.* by its source in a holy God. The source of an eternal faith can only moralise that faith if there be established at its centre with might what reigns in the universe by right—the moral majesty, the holiness of God. That is theology; but it is also essential Christianity, so far as a Church's witness is concerned. I am not speaking here about individual religion.

Yet so far have we got from this supreme concern of Christ, that when the effort is made to give it its true place for His work on earth, some minds, demoralised by their very religion, cry out against theology, and metaphysics, and academics. It is a cry charged with the ruin of the Christian future. There is nothing that need surprise us in the failure, the ebb, of any Church which treats the holiness of God as a piece of theology, and its centrality to the conscience as a piece of metaphysic. What is the worth to the Christian gospel of a piety which calls the theology of holiness academic? Protest as you like against the language of pure thought, and the inaccessibility to relative man of the unconditioned absolute in the ethic of pure thought. Protest strongly against making salvation depend on assent to the metaphysics of Trinity. But when we have come to be so saturated with the religious impressionism of the hour that an ultimate concern of heart, soul, and mind with the holiness of God is a strange tongue to us, when we call the satisfaction of that holiness a mere piece of theology, then the kid is seethed in its mother's milk, and the soul sodden with the very religion that should be its food. Of course most men, even religious men, are unfamiliar with the holiness of God, but the unfamiliar is not the academic.

We are paying bitterly now, and we shall pay more bitterly yet, in the bewilderment of our youth, for that neglect by the Church to educate its ministry in its own subject at the plastic time, which makes such talk possible. When preachers denounce theology, or a Church despises it for literary or social charm, that is to sell the cross to be a pendant at the neck of the handsome world. It is spiritual poverty and baldness, it is not the simplicity in Christ, to be sick of grace, judgment, atonement, and redemption. The holiness of God has become a spent force if a gospel which turns entirely upon it is called metaphysical or academic.

IV

Let us not be ashamed of the cross of Christ, for there alone the final and public righteousness of God is revealed to our growing faith. A moral order of the world is our one modern certainty, among those who are certain of anything. And if, as we Christians believe, this moral order reflects the nature of a holy God (without exhausting His being) then the supreme interest of the world lies there, in that God. All the bearings of an ethical faith like Christianity

therefore must be taken from there. Christianity is only true
if it deal with this, and it is only final if it come to final
terms with it. The cross of Christ has more than a passing
place only if it give final effect to this holy thing, and is
understood in relation to it. It has no meaning as an incident, none except as it is understood; none as a piece of
history, only as it is superhistoric. It is presented to our
conscience, and not to our sympathies or tastes. It is not
an impressive spectacle but a decisive act, with the moral
order of God's holiness for its central issue and first charge.
The application of this is the one thing needful for the
internal troubles of our religion to-day. An enlightened
Judaism can preach a gospel of forgiveness, but our Christian religion has primarily to do with the terms of forgiveness; not with God's readiness to forgive, but with His way
of redemption; not with His willingness, but with His will;
and with His will not merely as His aim, but as His deed;
not as intended, but as achieved. The feeble gospel preaches
"God is ready to forgive"; the mighty gospel preaches
"God has redeemed." It works not with forgiveness alone,
which would be mere futile amnesty, but with forgiveness in
a moral way, with holy forgiveness, a forgiveness which
not only restores the soul, but restores it in the only final and
eternal way, by restoring in the same act the infinite moral
order, and reconstructing mankind from the foundation of
a moral revolution. God reconciles by making Christ to be
sin, and not imputing it (2 Cor. v. 21). The Christian act
of forgiveness at once regards the whole wide moral order
of things, and goes deep to the springs of the human will
for entire repentance and a new order of obedience. This it
does by the consummation of God's *judgment* in the central
act of mercy. Do not think of God's judgment as an arbitrary
infliction, but as the necessary reaction to sin in a holy God.
There alone do you have the *divine* necessity of the cross
in a sinful world—the moral necessity of judgment. A
judgment upon man alone would have destroyed him. And
a judgment borne by God alone would be *manqué*, it would

be wide of the mark, as being irrelevant to man's experience and regeneration. But borne by God in man, in such a racial, nay cosmic, experience as the cross of Christ, it is the creation of a new conscience, and of the new ethic of the race. When Christ died, all died. Dying with Christ is not a mere ethical idea, complete only as we succeed in doing it. It is a religious or mystic idea, which is ethical as taking effect in a holy act, where, however, it is already complete in principle. It is not applying the principle of salvation to life; the foregone salvation becomes our life; and practical Christianity is freely living it out, and not merely squaring life to it laboriously. The judgment involved is one that fell on Christ once for all. It is not a judgment in individual men, but in man in Christ. It is not the sum total of our self-judgments under Christ's light; rather say, all our self-judgment is but inspired by the complete judgment on Christ once for all. It is on us according as we are in Him, yet not as a judgment, but as a grace; not as a punishment, but as salvation; not as a scourge, but as a cross.

Without such a cross and its Atonement we come to a religion of much point but no atmosphere, much sympathy and no imagination, much kindness and no greatness, much charm and no force—a religion for the well-disposed and not for the rebel, in which we love our neighbour, but not our enemy, and not our Judge; a religion for the sensitive, but not for the world. When the world-cross goes out of the centre of religion, religion in due time goes out of the centre of man's moral and public energy. The public then goes past the preacher because he is not strong enough to arrest and compel them. He has too much to say and too little to tell. He hangs to his age by its weakness, and not by its strength. He does not reach its soul with such gospel as he has. The pathos of Christ takes the place of his power. We canonise the weak things of our Christian world in our haste for rapid success with the many. Religion becomes too æsthetic, too exclusively sympathetic, too bland, too naturalistic. Our very Christmas becomes the festival of babyhood, Good Friday the worship of grief, and Easter of spring and renewal instead of regeneration. To use the old theological language, under an obsession of culture and its pensive delicacies we become dominated by the passive obedience of Christ instead of His active. We treat the cross as a passion only, instead of a principle, or as a moral principle instead of a decisive deed. Christ becomes a pathetic, tender, helpful and gracious figure rather than a mighty. We prefer the flavour of the evening service to that of the morning. The religion that is driven out of business and our energetic hours takes refuge in our tired hours and our evening time. And it takes on that hue. It acquires that passive type—even in the preachers too often, whose active business it should be. We tend to overprize the subdued, composed, and vespertinal type of religion, whose patron saints are outside the evangelical succession with Francis and Fra Angelico; or we are engrossed with the genial, brotherly, and bustling type. And all the time the Church is dropping into a vague Arianism: it is losing faith in the incarnation, faith in the real presence of the redeeming God, and therefore faith in a strenuous and historic ethic. Is it wonderful that it should be deploring a decline which it cannot stay by all its religious galvanism and its forced enterprises? The idea we are offered is a kingdom of man, with God to serve it, rather than a kingdom of God, with man to serve it. It is a consecration of the natural man *by* God instead of his redemption *to* God. It trusts to man's Christian culture instead of his conversion. The God within exploits the God without. The divinest humanity is aided by a most humane divinity. The historic facts of our faith become not so much unique organs of God's self-revelation, as means of making us aware of the good God within us, and living up to Him. We do not so much owe our soul to the fact of Christ; we impose on that fact the soul within us, the humane soul, crude, but still very capable, dim, but unlost; and so we really receive but what we give. Revelation is then not an objective authority, given at a point once for all; it is but a subjective way of treating history. The course of history is the real revelation. The deification of a point in it, of a person in it, is only a passing mythology, forced on us by a psychological necessity, though it may be very valuable when properly guarded. But Jesus cannot be regarded as an objective revelation. He lives while we believe.

The tendency to dwell upon the passive obedience of Christ is but the theological way of expressing the tendency to dwell on God's sympathy and to ignore His salvation. There is little doubt that the sympathetic tendency is the more popular to-day, and to press salvation in a real sense is to be accused of a reactionary bias to theology. But a God who is merely or mainly sympathetic is not the Christian God. The Father of an infinite benediction is not the Father of an infinite grace. We are often warned of the dangers of anthropomorphism, especially by those who are preoccupied with the superpersonal element in God. But what we need much more to-day is a caution against anthropopathism, or a conception of God which thinks of Him chiefly as the divine consummation of all our human pity and tenderness to man's mischance, bewilderment, sorrow and sin. A being of infinite pity would not rise to the height of the Christian God. And a religion of far more sympathy than we have yet felt would not be the Christian religion. It is needless to dwell on the preciousness of sympathy. The man who needs none is something less than human; and the man who receives none remains so. But a sympathy which has no help in it mocks us with an enlargement of our own sensitive impotence, which means so much better than it can. And yet a sympathy which could only help would not secure us against the fear that all its help might be at last in vain. It might not reach me, or not my worst need; or it might be arrested in some future by a power more mighty to foil than to help. We must have a sympathy that can not only help but save, save to the uttermost, save for ever, and not only bless but redeem. Nay, far more, we must have, for the entire confidence of faith, a sympathy that *has* redeemed, and already triumphs in a conclusive salvation. If God, indeed, could not sympathise, He would be less than God. There would be a region, large or small, into which He could not pass. There would be an insuperable obstacle set to Almighty God by a something which by so far reduced His power and resisted His access. He would be a limited being, tied up, as impersonal things are, by their own nature, and incapable of passing beyond it. But all the same, if God were all sympathy, if His divine power lay chiefly in His ability to infuse Himself with super-human intimacy of feeling into the most unspeakable tangles and crises of human life, then also He would be less than God, and we should have no more than what might be called a monism of heart. Even a loving God is really God not because He loves, but because He has power to subdue all things to the holiness of His love, and even sin itself to His love as redeeming grace. A sympathetic God is really God because He is a holy, saving, redeeming God; because in Him already the great world-transaction is done, and the kingdom of His holy love already set up on His foregone conquest of all evil. The great and crucial thing is done *in* God and not *before* Him, in His will and not in His presence, *by* Him and not *for* Him by any servants, not even by a son. It is an act of His own being, a victory in His own immutable and invincible being. And to be saved, in any non-egoistical sense of the word, means that God gains His own victory over again in me, and that I have lost in life's great issue unless He do. God's participation in man's affairs is much more than that of a fellow-sufferer on a divine scale, whose love can rise to a painless sympathy with pain. He not only perfectly understands our case and our problem, but He has morally, actively, finally solved it. The solution is for ever present with Him. Already He sees, and for ever sees, the travail of His soul and is *satisfied*. All the jars, collisions, contradictions, crises, pities, tragedies and terrors of life are in Him for ever adjusted in a peace

c

which is not resigned and quietist, but triumphant and exultant; and nothing can pluck us from His hands All history, through His great act at its moral centre, is, in God, resolved into the harmonies of a foregone and final conquest. And our faith is not merely that God is with us, nor that one day He will clear all things up and triumph; but that for Him all things are already triumphant, clear, and sure. All things are working together for good, as good is in the cross of Christ and its saving effect. Our faith is not that one day we shall solve the riddles of providence, and see all things put under us, but that now we see Jesus; and that we commit ourselves to one who has both the solution of every tragic thing and the glory of every dark thing clear and sure in a kingdom that cannot be moved, and, therefore alone, moves for ever on.

Our current religion of sympathy is but a section, and not the central or effectual section, of a religion which is a religion of redemption; and of achieved redemption, else it must at last cease to be a religion at all. That, and only that, is the fulness of the evangelical gospel.

But in all the subjectivism I have named are we not slowly passing to another religion, a religion which starts with man's spiritual nature and not with God's self-revelation, with humanity and not with history, where man becomes "his own Holy Ghost"? We are bidden to study human nature, not the Bible, not Jesus Christ, except to look there for classic cases of spiritual humanity and high prophetism. The Bible becomes then but a valuable deposit of that irrepressible spiritual energy in man which in every age takes its own form, and finds no kind of finality in any age. That, of course, reduces Jesus to a mere historic link instead of a perennial presence; and His cross to one of the crises we have surmounted, or are in process of doing so. The greatest personality is but a node in the great evolution. Man needs but evolution and not revolution. He only needs that his face be cleared, and not turned steadfastly to Jerusalem.

Let us see exactly where the point is, and let us be quite fair to the kind of liberal religion in view. It does not, of course, exclude God. It does not say that the religious development of man is a smooth or an automatic thing. Progress still needs the help of God, or whatever stands for God. It needs even the act of God. The origin of faith within man is an act of God. But the point is that this act is not a revolution in man, not a new creation, not a regeneration, not an absolute redemption, but only a release, an impulse from God, the extrication of our best, a delivery of the innate spirituality and goodness of man with which history is in travail until now. It is not a salvation from death but only from scanty life. There is no real critical life-and-death catastrophe in the moral history of the race; but what we have is a deep consistent progress, harmonious on the whole, each step attaching to the step before. We have the happy perfecting of those decent, just, or tender instincts which are the original righteousness of human nature, the gradual surmounting by moral culture of sense and self. God is our helper and no more. He is not in a real sense, but only in a figurative sense, our Redeemer. He helps us to realise our latent spiritual resources and ends. There is no break with self and the world, only a disengagement from an embarrassing situation.

It should be clear that this is another religion from that of redemption; and it has no room or need for atonement. And if it be true, then Christianity is not so necessary as we were led to think. Its whole complexion is changed. Nothing so very serious has taken place. Things can be bad enough, but not so bad as all that. Human nature is very mysterious but there is nothing marvellous, miraculous, in God's relation to it, nothing perilled on an eternal edge, nothing like a new creation, nothing that needs much penetration or agony of holy thought. Incarnation becomes a metaphor. These greatest words are felt so great and useful because they can be made to mean anything. Well, faith in the incarnation is bound to become a metaphor, and to sink, if we count it mere theology to take it seriously that God was in Christ reconciling the world, and to press on to understand the mighty God thus hallowed in the atoning cross. It is bound to sink, so as to become the incarnation of man instead of God, if in the cross we see but the extreme suffering of the most loving man instead of the supreme act and victory of the most holy God. If Christianity do not make a revolution in human nature we make a revolution in Christianity. A religion centring wholly in the graciousness of Christ, or His submission, or His spiritual insight can be no foundation for a commanding ethic or a triumphant faith. It lacks the virile note. Christ did not come as a grand spiritual personality, but as the Redeemer. It was not to spiritualise us that He came but to save us. Moral verve is bound to relax if the religion of the cross become but a hallowed addition to life's spiritual interests or touching moods, if it do not carry the stamp of moral crisis and personal decision for death or life. Ethic is bound to grow less strenuous, even while we bustle about ethical conduct, if the sublime ethical issue of the universe is not the marrow of our personal divinity and the principle of our personal religion. We can find a strong foundation only in that centre where the holy God both bears our load and performs His new creative act. If in the cross we have but the greatest of love's renunciations instead of the one establishment of God's holy will, if we have but the divine Kenosis and not also the divine Plerosis, then the sense of God's presence in the cross, and in the Church, and in the world's moral war, is bound to fade. The eternal ruling God cannot be a God in a passive or touching cross merely. A religion of simple service is no religion to rule a world like this. We shall come to feel that in such a cross, a cross that only stands for sacrifice, there is no God, but only a victory of God's foes, another and a tremendous case of the world crushing the good and just, another case of the soul's defeat by fate. Then, of course, Christianity must die. "The cross is either the life of our religion, or it is the death of all religion. Either it is the supreme atonement, and so the final guarantee of God's Fatherhood and its victory; or else it is a mere martyr death, and so an eclipse of that fatherhood, its greatest historic eclipse, which would mean its extinction." Christ would then have publicly trusted a God who did not publicly give Him the victory. Such a pathetic, mystic, and martyred Messiah could stir the sympathy of many, but He could not win the worship of the world. He could impress but not forgive; he could move men but not redeem them; he could criticise society but not judge the world. A king the world could just crucify is no king the world could fear; it needs a king who in his cross judged the world, and did not simply find his fate there. There is nothing central, nothing creative for life in such a fate. There may be much in it to appeal to our sympathetic and religious side, but nothing to establish faith, nothing to ethicise it for ever from a creative centre, nothing to fortify us against the unholy, nothing to set conscience and holiness on the throne of the world. If Christ died to saving and central purpose, then He died as the act of God. His death was God's act in the sense that it was the moral activity of God. God was in Christ and His death, acting there, setting up an everlasting kingdom, and not simply inflicting a racial penalty, nor simply suffering a racial fate.

Moreover, a pathetic cross sends our active sympathies mainly to Christ's teaching and His miracles. If we see in Christ and His cross chiefly the passive and the affecting side, and not the active and creative side; if we see Christ's love enduring judgment more than God's holiness triumphant in judgment and doing in it the grand, nay, the one moral act of the world; if we see but that endurance, no wonder the active vigorous world turns away from the cross to the teaching of Christ and His beneficence. For these *are* acts of will, positive deeds with active beneficent effect. It is no wonder a cross of pathetic and appealing suffering, a cross of mere sacrifice, should become decentralised in favour of these. But these have no permanent value for us in themselves, but only as expressions of Christ's person. The great thing is not that they were said or done, but said or done *by Him*. And yet they were not great enough to be an adequate expression of a person so mighty. And the person of Christ would be dumb and inert for us in the world's last crisis, apart from its active assertion and cosmic triumph on the cross. The cross, therefore, was no martyr passivity of the finest prophet, led like a lamb to the slaughter; it was the work of a Messiah king with power over Himself. Christ never merely accepted His fate; He willed it. He went to death as a king. It was the supreme exercise of His royal self-disposal. The same great picture which presents the sheep before the shearers dumb deepens before its close to one who poured out His soul unto death. And when we obscure that, when we pity where we should worship, melt where we should kneel, or kneel where we should rise to newness of life, it is no wonder if faith become a mere affection, or a mere ethical ritual of conduct, and cease to be the absolute committal of ourselves to communion with Him for ever. It is no wonder then if it cease to be the practical and eternal consignment of our spirit into His hands who has redeemed us as our Lord God of Truth. Faith is really self-disposal. But currently it is not. It is any one of a multitude of things, but not that, except in some feeble or breezy sense which does not save the moral asthenia of the Church. The Church has lost much moral tone even in its occupation with ethical subjects. And why? It has lost power to guide the instinct of self-sacrifice when it reduces the cross to nothing else. Has it not lost religious weight in the weightiest matters with the weightiest people? And the deep cause is its modern failure to understand the cross, to see in the judgment of the cross God's righteousness, God's holiness, coming finally to its own, and to realise this as the one object for which man exists or the world. This failure is bound to tell when acting on the scale of a Church, however secure many fine souls may feel living in a coterie and painting angels in their solitary cells.

It is only as God's act, then, that Christ's death can regain or retain a central place in faith. Second, it is only as an act revolutionary for man. And farther, it is only as an act in which His holiness gives the law to His love, and judgment makes grace precious. Holiness must be the first charge on the Saviour. If we spoke less about God's love and more about His holiness, more about His judgment, we should say much more when we did speak of His love. And we should keep that supreme in our faith which was supreme in Christ's, in that saving hour when the sense of love was dimmed, when communion failed, and nothing was left but faith by which to save the world.

It is round this sanctuary that the great camp is set and the great battle really waged. Questions about immanence may concern philosophers. And questions about miracles may agitate physicists. But the great dividing issue for the soul is neither the Bethlehem cradle nor the empty grave, nor the Bible, nor the social question. For the Church at least (however it be with individuals) it is the question of a redeeming atonement. It is here that the evangelical issue lies. It is here, and not upon the nativity, that we part company with the Unitarians. It is here that the unsure may test their crypto-unitarianism. I would unchurch none. I would but clear the issue for the honest conscience. It is this that determines whether a man is Unitarian or Evangelical, and it is this that should guide his conscience as to his ecclesiastical associations. Only if he hold that in the atoning cross of Christ the world was redeemed by holy God once for all, that there, and only there, sin was judged and broken, that there and only there the race was reconciled and has its access to the face and grace of God—only then has he the genius and the plerophory of the Gospel. If he hold to Christ on this head, then, whatever views he may hold on other heads, he is of the Gospel company and the Evangelical pale. Only thus has he a real final message for the age, Only thus is he more than one that has a lovely voice and can play well on an instrument for the ages' pleasure—and its final neglect.

II

SO THE ATONING CROSS IS
CENTRAL TO THE NEW TESTAMENT GOSPEL.
BUT IT IS CENTRAL ALSO TO
CHRISTIAN EXPERIENCE

I

THERE are two sets of admissions that should be made after what I have said. One concerns the history of the doctrine, the other concerns its place in individual experience.

(1)

As to the doctrine in history, we ought to admit the value of much of the socinian and rationalist criticism of it. The value is negative and corrective, but it is value. The ecclesiastical form of the doctrine is the source of most of the prejudice against it. And I mean particularly the forms it took among the Protestant scholastics of the 17th century. Many of these forms will not bear the light of Scripture any more than of reason. They are more aristotelian than apostolic. I do not say they depart from the New Testament doctrine, because it would be hard in the present position of New Testament knowledge to say the New Testament had a complete doctrine. But it has a principle and a norm which is positive enough to enable us to rule out many notions which misrepresent God's grace. For instance, we can no longer treat the atonement as a deflection of God's anger, as if the flash fell on Christ and was conducted by Him to the ground, while we stood in passive safety, with no part or lot in the incomprehensible process. We can no longer speak of a strife of attributes in God the Father, justice set against mercy, and judgment against grace, till an adjustment was effected by the Son. There can be no talk of any mollification of God, or any inducement whatever, offered by either man or some third party, to procure grace. Procured grace is a contradiction in terms. The atone ment did not procure grace, it flowed from grace. What was historically offered to God was also eternally offered by God, within the Godhead's unity. The Redeemer was God's gift. Farther, we must not think that the value of the atonement lies in any equivalent suffering. Indeed, it does not lie in the suffering at all, but in the obedience, the holiness.[1] It is both a moral and a psychological impossibility that an amount of suffering equivalent to what we deserved should ever have been undergone by Christ or any holy personality in our stead. Again, we must speak very differently about the transfer of guilt; and never as if it were a ledger amount which could be shifted about by divine finance, or a ponder- able load lifted to another back. We have to be cautious in using the word penalty in connection with what fell on Christ. We must renounce the idea that He was punished by the God who was ever well pleased with His beloved Son. The chastisement of our peace was upon Him indeed; He entered the penumbra of our penalty; but if we think there is no chastisement left for us when we are in Him, we have against that idea the whole classic Christian experience, which finds the truest, deepest, and bitterest repentance in the course or end of the Christian life rather than at the beginning. But it is one of our present misfortunes that so much criticism of the popular doctrine with its abuse of repentance, is conducted by people who seem not to know what bitter repentance, spiritual brokenness and total humiliation mean. I would rather repent truly with a Salvationist theology than criticise that theology with a judicial superiority which needs no repentance.

(2)

But in respect of personal experience, do we deny all true faith which does not grasp the atoning cross? Surely not; so long as that cross is not denied or denounced; and

[1] I develop this later in the closing chapter.

so long as the experience of particular individuals is not made the measure of the message of the Church.

I hope I take due account of the effect of Christ's person, word, and deed upon individuals before the cross. I often recall Zaccheus, the Magdalen, Peter, and, I may add, Judas. And to-day still the life, the words, the acts, the death of Christ have a precious power to rouse men, to break, heal, and restore them to Him, without direct reference to His atoning work. The saving action of Christ for many individuals begins there—in His life, and especially to-day; and it only attains late unto the resurrection from the dead. We do ill to force the ripe experience of the cross on those who can as yet feel but its dawn. Any theology of atonement must be adjusted to the indubitable fact that Christ's forgiveness may and does reach personal cases apart from conscious reliance on His atoning work, or grasp of its theology. To do otherwise would be to show ourselves the victims of a pedantic dogmatism or a theological papacy. To preach Christ is indeed fundamentally to preach His atonement; but it is not incessantly to preach about it. We must always preach it, but we need not always preach about it. Only it must not be denied or denounced, never ignored or levelled down to the category of man's efforts to atone his own sins. It is true there are historic stages and junctures when to preach Christ in the more theological form is the only preaching relevant to the mental and moral situation. It was so at the Reformation. But to-day it may be more needful in certain positions to preach the Christ of the cross than the cross of Christ. There is a strategy in the holy war. It is the last crisis that calls the reserves to the front. But whether we preach the Christ who atoned or the atonement of Christ it is still an atoning Christ and an atoning cross we preach. To preach only the atonement, the death apart from the life, or only the person of Christ, the life apart from the death, or only the teaching of Christ, His words apart from His life, may be all equally one-sided, and extreme to falsity.

I will only stop to remark here that the more the conscience is affected by Christ's words or behaviour, the more is that standard generated within us which demands the atonement in the cross. It was the Christ of the latent cross that said these words, and did these things. It was the Christ who Himself was driven by His experience to recognise that the crowning thing He came for was to die. And another remark must be made. What we are chiefly concerned with is the great message and experience of the Church; and that cannot be whittled down to the experience of individuals and their early stages. It is a minimal gospel, set on numbers, that is paralysing the cross. Preach the total Christ therefore in the perspective of evangelical faith, but with immediate stress on that aspect most required by the conscience of the hour. For the Reformation age the ethical concern may have been satisfaction and its true form; for our age, with another public ethic, it may be judgment as the demand of a social righteousness. For that age the interest was far more directly theological and juristic, now it is more psychological and ethical. Then it was the Christ of the two natures cohering in one person that gave value to the cross, now the stress is the Christ of the one, holy, obedient personality. The unity we prize in the Saviour is one realised not metaphysically but personally, a unity by and in the cross as the crowning moral act both of God and of humanity in Christ. But a point of unity we must seek if our faith is to be unified, if life is to be unified out of its present distraction, if religion is to have a vital core, and cease to be a frame of pious moods or morals. Our relation to God must be a real one and not subjective. It must turn on a positive fact and act, which gives it both reality and unity; and on a fact of history. It is not enough to say this fact is the person of Christ. If His be not a mere loose-hung personality, with a religious casualism, just doing perfectly whatever turned up each day, the person must itself have a principle of unity. This principle cannot, with our data about Him, be psychological; even with more data, perhaps, it would still be beyond our comprehension psychologically. "Du gleichst dem Geist den du begreifst nicht mir." But it is a theological unity, converging on His death and the consummation there of all that made His person what it was, all that took Him out of the category of other men, and made the ground of our salvation. He saved us by His difference from us. He did not redeem us because He represented us; rather He represents us because He redeemed. It is true He could not redeem man without representing him. But had He redeemed man by only representing him, man would be self-redeemed in the human classic. It is the atoning death of Christ as the representative of God in man that makes Jesus a complete and closed personality with a final action on the world. It is the offering to God in man of a holiness possible only to God. He died once for all, the just for the unjust, that He might bring us to His finality of God.

II

But after these admissions let me lay the more stress on the necessity of this atonement for that maturer Christian experience which gives us the true type of faith.

The conscience has many functions, and the atonement of Christ satisfies or stirs them all. It strikes light from many angles, and it is presented in the New Testament in various complementary ways. But its chief action on the conscience is to pacify its accusations with the love and grace of God. Faith is above all the life of a conscience. It is the life of a conscience which is stilled and established by the forgiveness of God in the faith that there is now no condemnation. True enough, as I have said, this may take a real, though an incipient form, in the deep impression made by the tender mercy of the kindly Christ. But many never rise above this level. It is enough for them to respond to Christ's gracious way with the sinners He met. They place themselves among the sinners He forgave and healed during His life. They do not ask where He places them. To some He was not healing but severe. And they may question the need of any atonement. The assurance from Christ of God's forgiveness is enough for them. But that is a very naïve and all too simple faith for such a conscience as ours, and such a world. Let its value for certain individuals not be denied. Who would be exacting with the simple souls? But surely it condemns them to be perpetual moral minors. And it keeps faith at the lay level. Ours is indeed a lay faith, but the Church could not live on it at lay level. If such people go on to think and ask questions (as they should for their soul's life), in passing from disciples to regenerates, must they not begin to have certain misgivings? (Bachmann.) Must they not, for instance, say to themselves at some time: "Those cases that Jesus forgave were but single cases; is mine quite parallel? If He forgave them must He also forgive me? Is God's forgiveness just a series of acts, one for each soul? If so how do I know where they may stop, whether they will reach to me? How shall I realise that His forgiveness is one great racial act into which I am built, so that when one died all died and all were redeemed?" Moreover, the soul goes on to think thus: "As I grow in Christ my sin grows on me, and the tremendous thing in my pardon grows on me. The damnability of my sin grows on me, and with it the incredibility of grace. How do I know not merely that God is willing to forgive but that He has forgiven, that what is so incredible is equally unalterable?" Still farther. The believer sins after he has been forgiven. "Am I fit," he says in his repentance, "to stand with those that Jesus forgave? They did not betray Him. I have sinned against a light and an experience they never had. I am a chief of sinners. I have sinned my mercy." Moreover, there rises on his soul a deepened sense of Christ's demand. His forgiving words to special cases lose force compared with the exigence of His general demand and the holiness of His standard. His judgment grows more serious than it seemed in our first forgiveness. How shall we stand? Better people than we He

left outside His kingdom. And so we oscillate between the
goodness and the severity of God. We are tossed from the
one to the other. They alternate as it were according to our
mood, they are not entwined and fused. They thwart each
other, and get in each other's way; they do not sustain each
other. And the conscience finds no rest till it find in the
cross the one final act in which both are reconciled and
inwoven, with the grace uppermost. I meet the atonement
where the sin of the whole world is taken away, which
carries in it the foregone forgiveness of sins that I dread
and yet am sure I shall do. There are various ways in which
a man finds it hard to take home the forgiveness he craves
by a general declaration of God's love. Some may not feel
so much the greatness of their sin as the incredibility of
anything so vast as God's love. There may not be grievous
blots on their life, yet they feel that the state of the world's
conscience must call out God's judgment on the race,
including them. On the other hand if there be such blots in
life, and especially if a man sins after his forgiveness in a
grievous way, he gets such a shock in the revelation of sin's
tough and subtle power that it needs something very final
and decisive to assure him of its destruction. He must then
have a grace which is not simple and self-evident—for
"lightly come, lightly go." He must have a finished work,
and a God who has made a full end. A conscience in his
state, as soon as it thinks on a world scale, must have a grace
and salvation which is not benignant only, but gathers up
the total moral situation in one act, and settles the great
strife for good and all. He must have more than a full
forgiveness, he must have a complete redemption. And
that means one that pursues, captures, and subdues to
God's holy purpose those consequences of our sin also
which have long gone beyond our control or knowledge,
and are out on the world doing evil work at compound
interest on their own account. A man needs something to
make him confident that his past sin, and the sin he is yet
sure to commit, are all taken up into God's redemption,

and the great transaction of his moral life is done. The real complete forgiveness is the appropriation of the world's atonement.

It is not easy. Theological belief may not be so hard. But for a man to make Christ's atonement the sole centre of his moral life, or of his hope for the race, is not easy. Nothing is so resented by the natural self as the hearty admission of man's native lostness and helplessness, especially when he thinks of all the heroisms, integrities, and charities which ennoble the race. It is not always pride, it is often a mere natural self-affirmation. It is a native self-respect, which makes him shrink from submitting himself absolutely to the judgment of another. Even in his repentance he does not want to lose all self-respect. He feels he cannot amend the life of conscience, and repair the old faults, without some remnant of self-respect to work from. His new shoots must come from the old stump, which must not be rooted out. He is fighting for the one remnant of a moral nature which if he lost he fears he would be less than a man. He does not easily realise what a poor thing his self-justification must be compared with his justification by God, his self-repair beside God's new creation. He does not feel how sterile the stump is, how poorly his moral remnant would serve him for his moral need, how that recuperative vitality is the one thing he lacks, how absolute God's grace is, and how complete is the moral re-creation in Christ. He palters with a synergism which is always trying to do the best for human nature in a bargain with God. And he does not realise how this starves and pinches the conscience itself, compared with the moral fulness of a total gift of grace and a new man in Jesus Christ. There are thus a thousand influences of no quite ignoble sort which may arrest a man's total committal of himself and his kind to the new creation in Christ's cross. And it seems a reasonable self-respect which solicits him to reserve a plot of freehold in his interior where his house is his castle, and he can call his soul his own, even at the challenge of the holy and all-searching Judge. He does not, perhaps, venture to say that God and the soul are co-equal foci in the moral ellipse, but he struggles, sometimes pathetically, to set up what is as impossible morally as mathematically—a subsidiary centre; which is a contradiction in terms. There is but one centre, one Lord, one cross, one faith, and one spirit of a new life in Christ Jesus.

III

It has been asked concerning Christ, Was His will to die one with His will to save? Is there any doubt about the answer the Church has given to that question from first to last? The salvation has always been attached to Christ's death, from New Testament days downward. This has not indeed passed without challenge, especially in recent times; but the challenge has not affected the catholicity and continuity of the Church's witness as a whole to that truth of its foundation. And the salvation is attached not to Christ's death as an incident of history or even as an object lesson of grace, but as the effectuation of grace—not, indeed, its procuring but its achievement, its putting in action. It is not the fact of Christ's crucifixion that saves, but the inner nature of that fact as understood, and not simply swallowed, by faith, understood as the atonement which makes reconciliation possible (2 Cor. v. 19-21). Such is the witness of you may say the whole Church about its central relation to its creator, its living tenant, and perpetual Lord.

But this suggests a serious question. It is declared that, if we be true to the true Christ of the Gospels, we shall relegate a final atonement in the cross to the region of those apostolic theologoumena, which like an evil weed seized and held the Church in a fatal plexus for so long. That means that Jesus did not understand His will to save to be one with His will to die. His death was either an arrest of His saving work, or an otiose sequel to it. It was a mere anecdote of His life, not its *dénouement*. And the serious question that then results is this, How came such a teacher, such a prophet, to be so deeply, so long, and so continuously misunderstood? If Christ's atoning death is not the central effect of His person, and the central thing to our faith, if that notion of atonement has overlaid Christ's real gospel, how has the whole Church come totally to misread its creator, and to miss what for Him *was* central? There has surely been some gigantic bungling on the Church's part, some almost fatuous misconception of its Lord, a blunder whose long life and immense moral effect is quite unintelligible. An error of that kind is no misprint but a flaw. It is not mistake but heresy. And, as it concerns the centre and nature of faith, it must destroy any belief in the guidance of the Church by the Holy Spirit—which, however, is not a very lively faith among those whose challenge here occupies us.

But leaving that, I will keep the question upon lines which represent a less doctrinal interest. What a poor thing human nature must be to have been affected so mightily, nay in a great measure revolutionised, by a mistake so deep and complete. What a poor and untrustworthy thing human nature must be, to have found in such a moral blunder the charter of a new ethic, the foundation of a new humanity, and the secret of eternal life. The Church has done its Lord many a wrong, but none so grave as this, to have determinedly perverted His legacy, and grieved His spirit in regard to the central object of His mission on earth. It has often travestied His methods, misconstrued points of His teaching, and even compromised His principles; but these things have been done against its best conscience and its holiest spirits. These errors have passed, and been reformed, and renounced. But this perversion I speak of, if perversion it be, is greater than these, less culpable possibly, but even greater as a perversion. For it has been the misrepresentation of Christ's central gospel by the Church's best and wisest. It has been a more total and venerable perversion than even the papacy. For even had all such passing ills and historic abuses been cured, this travesty of Christ's central intent would still have gone on, and gone on with all the force lent by a purified Church, and all the spell of saintliness to wing the central lie. If the cross was but little to Christ in comparison with His real work, if it was a mere by-product of His mission, a mere appendix to it and not its purpose, a mere calamity that befell it and not its consummation; and if His Church has yet made it central, seminal, creative, and submersive of all else, then the enemies who swore Christ's life away did Him no such bad turn as the train of disciples whose stupidity has belied Him over the whole world for all time. And those browbeaters who would let Him say nothing did His cause less harm than these apostles who made Him say what He did not mean.[1]

But we cannot stop here. There is worse to follow. What was Jesus about to leave such a blunder possible? What a *gauche* Saviour! What a clumsy teacher! How awkward a prophet! How unfinished with the work given Him to do!

---

[1] I would here anticipate a remark that may occur to some to the effect that I am allowing too much to the authority of the Church, and that if the arguments I apply in respect of the nature of redemption were applied to polity we should be delivered into the hands of Rome and an episcopal succession. In reply I would point out that the Church stands to the nature of its generative redemption in a relation quite different from that which it has to every other doctrine. It was the one thing that created the Church, and therefore the Church's verdict upon it has an authority quite interior and superior to her views on all besides. We may take the constitution of the Church, the ritual of the Church, or its theological system at any stage; and not one of these has the same creative relation to the Church as Christ's atoning death. We may even select from the system of Catholic truth the doctrine of the Incarnation. That truth, central as many find it, has no such centrality as the principle of atoning forgiveness. The doctrine of the Incarnation did not create the Church; it grew up (very quickly) in the Church out of the doctrine of the cross which did create it—in so far as that can be said of any doctrine, and not rather of the act and power which the doctrine tries to state. The doctrine of the Incarnation grew upon the Church out of its experience of Atonement. The Church was forced on the deity of Christ to account for its redeemed existence in Christ. We can experience the redemption as we cannot the incarnation. I have already said that the soterology sprang from soteriology—the creed of the person grew up in a Church which had been created by the experience of his salvation. The authority of the Church, therefore, in respect of the manner of its salvation is primary compared with its authority in regard to the constitution of its Saviour; and far

Regard it. Suppose the central thing committed by the Father to Christ's charge was not the atoning task; suppose He Himself is not central to His own Gospel, yet He departs and leaves a body of disciples who do believe His atonement to be the great work, and His person their God. And these have grown and spread into a Catholic Church, which, amid many distractions and divisions, still founds upon this evangelical rock, and is the greatest product of humanity. Well, I say, if there be this central perversion of Him by the body of His disciples and apostles, first and last, then and now, what are we to think of Him? If He so discharged His real mission from God, and so gave His message during three years of public and responsible life, that a central misunderstanding at once swamped that message as He really meant it, and smothered His word in His cross, what kind of testimony was that He bore, and with what face would He return to Him that sent Him? If His cross cost Him not only His life but His mission, His true message from God, and if His holiest apostles of the cross have been among the most active obscurantists of His

more in respect of its polity or its practice. Its testimony as to the cross is its witness to its own life. Here Loisy is right enough. There is a *continuum* in the Church which takes precedence of every specific view the Church may hold. It is the continuous, super-natural, eternal life. Only that life is not an indefinite vitality, without feature or content, and capable of almost any. But it is life as the new creation, carrying in its very heart its mark of origin, and having the seal of proceeding from the cross as the action of God's holy love on sinful man. My point then would be this. As the witness of an illiterate saint to God's grace in the redemption which has made him what he is has a value for the objective nature of that redemption that belongs to no other piece of his theology, so with the large testimony of the household of faith. Its witness to the divine act which called it into being and made it what it is, is on another footing from any matter of its polity or speculation. The Church might have gone widely wrong on grave points like these without wrecking its own existence; but to have gone so widely wrong on the point I am treating would be for the Church to commit suicide, to cease to be the thing that God once made, to cease witness to the Gospel that made it, and practically to deny the Lord that bought it. For that there would be no repentance. The Church of the papacy and the mass was reformable; but a Church that renounced universally its atoning redemption would not be reformable. It would be extinct, however long it kept the name to live. All turns on the cross (*i.e.* the total person of Christ put into the cross) being the power creative of the Church, and on the Church's relation and witness to this source and secret of its life.

real kingdom, surely when He consented, or even submitted, to death He signed away His commission, He consented too soon to die, He died before He had taught or secured His lesson, and He accepted the one thing that foiled His true intent. The hour that He should return to the Father was not ripe when He thought it was. Never did He think His death would be captured, exaggerated, and exploited like that to obscure the Father and the kingdom. I say, if He left His disciples convinced that a death which was to Him a side interest was His supreme bequest, and if the net result of His act all these ages has been to deepen and spread the mistake, then was He any fit trustee for the purpose of God? Observe this, too. The mistake is most deeply held and hallowed by those most near His own saintliness; its effect has been to generate that sanctity as nothing else has; and it is only discovered to be a mistake late in history, by men who, however good, have more sense of what is rational than of what is holy. Well, noting this, can you suppress the question whether sainthood to Christ is good service to God? If, I say, the saints nearest to Him have done most to decentralise in favour of the cross what was really dearest to Him; if His greatest cloud of witnesses becloud His real word, and help but as the crowd helps at a fire; if those who know they are saved only in His blood are in effect one with those who were guilty of His blood in silencing His real testimony—what are we to think of Him who so mismanaged things as to allow the blunder to be possible, who left His work in a condition that permanently spoiled it, and bequeathed to His best believers the doom of perverting the counsel of God?

Nay, farther, if the effect of Christ has been that the Church has worshipped a Redeemer on the cross when it should but have hearkened to God's prophet in His words, if it gave Him worship where it owed Him but attention, what must be the frame of mind in which He now lives and sees the misbirth that has come of the travail of His soul? If the Church was left by Him in such a state that it has gone on living on another centre than what was really His and God's, how shall we conceive the bitter regret with which He now views His old effort in the light of experience and of heaven? He who, we thought, had redeemed Israel botched the work, and left it to harden into a mere theology. And He who, we thought, ever lived to make intercession for us, must ever live in petition for Himself, that God would graciously forgive the well-meant failure He must sadly own. If the effect of the Church's evangelical faith upon Christ in heaven were to surprise and disappoint Him by its central note, then, before the Father, He would have to apologise for this diminution of *His* glory; He would have to lament that the work was not put into better hands, and given to one without the genius of being misunderstood most by those who loved Him best. And what before God He would have to confess for us, and deplore for Himself, would be not only the diminution of God's glory but its unhappy eclipse by His own. He has been taken and made a king in spite of Himself; and a king whose effect has been, not to hallow the Father's sole and suzerain name, but to obscure it by His own, to divide the worship and deflect the work of God.

I trust these thoughts will not be deemed extravagant. They are efforts to think to the end, and to think with the foundation of faith, the intelligence of conscience, and the experience of life. They are not the exercises of an ideologue. They are efforts to recall our minds to the actual crisis, to the need for concentration, decision, finality, and footing, to defend the Church from the university, to secure an evangelical faith against a faith but rational, to rescue the apostles from the apologists, and plead for a pistic creed against an academic. They are efforts, farthermore, to call in our minds from dawdling and dabbling in eternal things; to protect them from the current susceptibility, discursiveness, and distraction; to guard them from a too mobile sympathy, which answers every novelty, joins every society, reads the latest thing, and sows itself on every wind; to secure them from a morbid and dainty vivacity which has a brisk interest in everything, and may even reach a curiosity about the Eternal; to shelter our minds from the humane optimisms in which the devil whispers that devilry is dead and the perfection of manly culture is at hand. I would force our concern on one vast world issue in which time is won or lost for eternity, and the whole human soul for the all-holy God. We handle matters where to be right is to be right upon a final, sublime, and eternal scale. But to be wrong there is to fly from orbits of celestial range, and do damage at last to the inhabitants of heaven as well as the dwellers on earth. To be right here is to secure the Church's future, to be wrong here is to doom it. But for the Church to be right here is for the Church continually to cry "Holy, Holy, Holy, O Lamb of God, that takest away the sin of the world, have mercy upon us and grant us Thy salvation."

III

THE ATONEMENT CENTRAL TO THE
LEADING FEATURES OF MODERN
THOUGHT

I

THERE are several tendencies in the modern mind which seem to converge upon something more objective and central than that mind can itself provide. Humanity cannot explain itself. It does not carry in itself the chart of its own drift or the key of its own destiny. It moves to a point outside itself, to a point in God. The Christian creed says this point is in history, but not of it. It is the Kingdom of God in the cross of Christ. The crucifixion, of course, is a historic fact, like Jesus, but the cross, the Atonement, like the Christ, is superhistoric. And it is in this superhistoric consummation—the kingdom in the cross—that many of our finest modern aspirations should come to unity and rest.

These features are such as the passion for (1) unity of conception; (2) cosmic range; (3) social righteousness; (4) mercy, pity, and kindness.

1. There is no feature that more marks the mind of to-day than the craving for unity, and especially for unity of conception. It dominates the higher science; it is at the root of the hasty refuge some take in monism. It determines the higher Churchmanship; it inspires the search for a real authority. And it moulds the higher politics; it moves in the aspirations for brotherhood and the ambitions of democracy.

2. Nay, the passion for unity rises to a cosmic scale. Under the guidance of modern science we escape from abstract universals and we exult in cosmic realities and the cosmic imagination. Planetary systems are now more numerous than stars were once thought to be. Space not

only swells, but its distension is organised. And human destiny itself expands in proportion. The soul that renounces a historic God is yet invited to lose itself in a cosmic emotion or an enthusiasm of humanity. The all submerges the God of the all, the all-presence the All-Father, or the All-Father the God and Father of our Lord Jesus Christ.

3. With this goes the modern passion for righteousness—not merely for personal goodness, but for boundless good, for social righteousness. The demand grows for a recon-struction, a revolution if need be, of the social order in the interest of an ideal righteousness of no private interpretation. Public justice slowly but surely bears down private interests. It emerges more clearly as the dividing line between the two great parties. It seizes some people so vehemently that it becomes their religion; and personal religion wanes in consequence, and, with it, the membership of the Churches. There was never an age when the passion for public righteousness covered so many, or promised so much.

4. Add to this the humanitarian passion for mercy, pity, tenderness to the weak, consideration for life or suffering. You can get money for hospitals when you can get it for nothing else. The children of the community were never so cared for, and the young had never such chances. The submerged have at last emerged. We awake to the valuable products that can be extracted by new machinery from the wastage and wreckage of society. We have the politics of pity, or at least of sympathy—threatening at times even to swamp the politics of justice and the sanity of law. There is, of course, much that points the other way still, but there never was so much pointing that way, the way of mercy, pity, and love.

Take such features, then, as these alone—the passion for a unity or a centre, the passion for righteousness, especially social righteousness, the passion of sympathy or pity, and the passion which moves to conceive of such things on a cosmic scale. And then consider, on the other hand, the increased confusion in life, the loss of a centre of unity, the disagreement about the form of righteousness, the inadequacy of philanthropy, the sense of oppression by the vastitude of the cosmos. Take all the moral confusion and the soul-schism which lead first to deliberate yet passionate pessimism in the midst of our conquest of the world, and then to the settled despair which multiplies suicide. It is an age of very great spiritual derangement and moral dissolution, in spite of its spiritual instincts and ethical ardours. And to this confusion is offered by the Church the threefold unity of the cross—the holy love and grace of God, the saving judgment on sin, and the new Humanity. My interpretation is that those great groping lines of social tendency I named above draw together to this point, which history provides but not history alone, nor can mere humanity explain it. They find their focus in God's act of Christ's cross—where they not only meet and blend, but where they are fused and vitalised for a new future in the one burning centre of man and the world and God. The cosmic passion (2) of a merciful (4) justice (3) at the heart of the whole world (1) is realised only in the cross as the crowning act of a holy and gracious God—a God holy because He is the whole goodness of existence, and gracious because of the merciful love with which He goes out to save us into His own holiness.

1. To take the matter of unity. This cross will appear and remain the central issue of Christian doctrine only if it can be shown to be central to the ethic of the soul and of the race. It is only central to faith because it is central to conscience, and to the dramatic conscience of the race, nay, of God. What is the Atonement but the satisfaction of the conscience—God's and man's—the adjustment, the pacification, of conscience, and especially God's? It is the core of our religion, because it is the crisis of man's moral drama and the solution of that moral tragedy which is his collision with the holy. "Pain," says a fine literary critic in speaking of lyric art, "cannot be conquered till it is expressed." This is still more true of evil. Sin could not be conquered till it

was expressed. And that was what Christ did in God and God in Christ. He brought evil to a moral head and dealt with it as a unity. He forced a final crisis of the universal conscience to decide it for good. He forced battle unto victory once for all, for the race and for eternity. So we have here the burning focus of the great ethic of mankind. The great ethic! Some men miss that unity, that central issue, for lack of sensibility to the great ethic. They may have much ethical fervour and insight in questions of personal casuistry, sectional ethics, or social righteousness. Others miss its poignancy, for all they are masters of its history in thought. "It is strange how often men who brilliantly describe the ideas of history are quite unable to gauge the spiritual phenomena of their present." But all ethics or civics are affairs of less range and depth than the last moral juncture and final destiny of the total race, with which the great prophets and dramatists are concerned. All our collectivisms are but sectional within the grand moral crisis of collective Humanity. And more and more to-day we are impressed with two things—with the problem and destiny of Humanity as one, and with that issue as above all things moral in its nature. The whole social problem is at bottom a moral problem. And the moral problem is at bottom religious. It turns not merely upon man's normal or ideal state but upon his actual moral relation to God and God's personal unity of holiness. And religion ceases in the end to be moral if it become more of an evolution than a crisis, a dilemma, and a choice.

Have you read Thomas Hardy's great work *The Dynasts?* Have you marked here as elsewhere his apotheosis of a huge, blind, blundering force, which he dare not call He, behind man and the world? But surely the elemental energy which suffuses a race like ours with a central ethical genius, however stunted, can be no mere brutal It. Surely it must be a God, an ethical God, a holy God. If man be a He and God be an It, then man is his own God. And what must be the moral end of a self-idolatrous Humanity, of a

Napoleonine humanity? What can men do there but bite and devour one another, red in tooth and claw? But after all, the first, last, and supreme question of the soul, of religion when it is practical, is not, "How am I to think of God?—He or It?" but it is, "What does He think of me? How does It treat me?" More positively it is, "How shall I be just with God? How shall I stand before my judge?" That is the final human question—how to face the eternal moral power. What is it making of us? What is He doing with us? What is He going to do? That is the issue in all issues. That question of judgment is where all other questions end. It is the central question in religion, How shall I stand before my judge? So much is this the case, so inevitable, capital, and final is this function of judgment, that if God be not owned as man's judge, man becomes God's. Where man is not felt to be on his trial before God, God is put on His trial before man, and summoned to explain Himself to the conscience of the time.

> They talk to us so of an immanent God
>   As if man were the true Transcendent;
> As if man were the judge of all the Earth,
>   And God the poor defendant.
> As if God were arraigned with a very black case,
>   On the skill of his bar dependent,
> And "I wouldn't like to be God," says one,
>   "For his record is not resplendent."[1]

More and more we are driven to see this, as the interests of life grow less academic and more active, less philosophic and more ethical, less speculative and more practical, less artificial and more real. Here is the goal of all that drift to Realism, for which, on the whole, we have to be so thankful to-day. The last reality, and that with which every man willy-nilly has to do, is not a reality of thought, but of life and of conscience, and of judgment. We are in the world to act and take the consequences. Action means and matters everything in the world. It occurs in a world constructed for action and for judgment upon it. The question is not

[1] It is some reminiscence that I have cast into these lines.

about our views; nor is it about our subjective state—how do I feel? but of our objective relation—how do I stand? And it is the relation of a will to a will, a conscience to a conscience, unless the foundation and goal of life is non-moral. The last reality is a moral reality—unless life's morality is by-play; which, to its honour, English scepticism does not believe. It has to do with a moral situation, with the moral position of the soul to the race and the race to whatever stands for God. There lies the real unity of life. It is the question of the conscience and its Lord, of sin and righteousness, of the unholy and the holy. The net and total drift of human concern bears us down more and more remorselessly on that central issue. Society, in so far as it acts at all, or is concerned about worthy action, is being driven most reluctantly, amid violent and even hysterical resistance, to that ultimate ethical crux, where the theologians are waiting for it (themselves with a changed and softened temper) round the cross of Christ.

II

One of the favourite topics for discussion, amongst people who still discuss such things, is the question: "Is religion necessary for morality?" There never was a time when society as a whole cared so much for conduct as at the present day.[1] People are more agreed on the necessity of morality than on the necessity for religion. Yet with all this interest in morality on the part of both heterodox and orthodox, there is a frequent incapacity for handling moral ideas with insight and power. This age has more interest in moral subjects than capacity for handling moral ideas, more taste for ethics than faculty. The modern habit of thinking, keen as it is on moral topics, has lost the knack of dealing with moral realities; the only order of ideas where it seems at home is the region of the physical sciences, the measuring and observing sciences of matter and of force. Even psychology sinks to experiment and mensuration, and passes from

[1] 1909.

the study to the laboratory. And the mind so bred brings its habitual methods to bear on metaphysics and the social sciences, on morals, and history with much confidence. But those methods do not fit the case; and within the last few years the scientific mind itself has grown more conscious of their inadequacy. Philosophy must take up the work which empirical science has to lay down; and philosophy in turn must abandon its greatest matter to ethics, and for the purposes of life leave speculative for moral methods. We cannot deal with the ideas of the higher mathematics by the methods that serve us so well among the lower organisms. If we have to examine such a thing as moral freedom, we cannot simply bring to bear on the quest the methods which served in dealing with the expansion of gases. So also if we apply to historical development only the principles which regulate legal documents we do not treat the subject fairly. Very much depends on putting the right questions. And one notices with regret the occasional inability of some able minds to interrogate aright the moral man. When the conscience is questioned by congenial methods, and by a mind versed and apt in moral ideas, there is a voice and a verdict in it quite unheard by the ear that has only been refined to measure the tickings of an astronomical clock. There is the delicacy of sympathy and there is that of observation; and moral questions demand sympathetic treatment. Moral matters are inward, not outward. Outward observation may register the consequences of a moral act, but it cannot grasp the inner character, the nature and process of the moral act itself. It is motive that finally determines morality, not consequence; and motive is something to be gauged only by an inward and sympathetic eye. I can judge your acts, which are mere expressions, far more easily and safely than I can judge you, who are a person and a soul. I can guess or observe the results of your action far more easily than I can divine the motives you had in doing it. Yet these alone give it true moral value. Politics are utilitarian but ethics are not. We are not as much at home in the study of the soul as we are in the study of the brain; and we are more backward in reading the living conscience than in reading the exploits of past conscience in politics or history. We feel the importance of morality for outward society, but we do not interpret well its testimony to inward and spiritual realities. We are more agreed about right acts than upon what makes a right soul. We are ready to make greater sacrifices for our outward freedom, our individual freedom among men, than for our true moral freedom with God. We prize morality as a dealer might prize a Turner, not as a Ruskin would; we prize it for what it will fetch, the advantages it may be reckoned to bring for social or individual well-being, rather than its value to God. We even say that sin is an injury only to man and not to God. The strange, unstable conjunction of the age is the co-existence of a high morality with a lowered sense of a living God. Conscience has become a finger-post more than a voice; it points, but does not speak to us; it directs, but does not reveal.

Let us be heartily thankful for this general respect paid to morality. It is a good thing to have, and a clear gain upon sheer selfishness and pagan worldliness. But let us welcome it also on higher grounds. Our souls' destiny in life is independent of philosophy or science for its foundations. It stands rooted in our conscience, whether our private or social conscience. Only let society confess the primacy of conscience, and provided thought be free, it is a mere matter of time till it declare the supremacy of God. If conscience is an absolute social need, God cannot remain a mere social luxury. For, whether morality involves religion or not, conscience involves God; and under His guidance it will evolve Him before all eyes.

I would bear you back upon your own conscience, and bid you listen to its voice. Our moral coinage, whose is its image and superscription? We must have a common starting ground. Man is more than a consciousness, he is a conscience. He is not only aware of himself, he is critical of himself. There is in the soul a bar, a tribunal; our thoughts and actions are ranged before it; judgment is passed there upon what we have been and done. Every one who believes in morality believes in the conscience as the power we have of passing moral judgment upon ourselves. Talk of public opinion! What is it in severity and power to private opinion —a man's most private opinion of himself? And we treat him—our judicial self—with much respect. His praise will carry us a long way; his censure cast us down. It will divide and set us against ourselves, and destroy the joy in every other part of us. We fear this judge, this critic, in our own heart; we go as far, at times, as to hate him. If we could get at him we would put him out of the way. We would bribe him. And we even try that, but always with incomplete success. We would blind him, throw dust in his eyes, sophisticate him; and that is partially successful at times. We would kill him, and that we think sometimes we do. But we wake up to find it is a delusion, and he has been fooling us. Some have even tried, having failed in every other way, to kill this voice by killing themselves; but there has never been any certainty that this was a success. "For in that sleep of death what dreams may come must give us pause." And we have an uneasy surmise that the dream beyond may be worse than the waking here, that there is a self we cannot kill, that the persecuting voice only reappears after the silence in another quarter, like the subterranean ghost of Hamlet's father, who made a conscience for him. We cannot get rid of this judge. He is not in our power. We cannot unmake him, though he be against ourselves. Then we did not make him. He is an incorporate part of our own being, our other self wedded to us for ever. What a strange thing we are—two, yet one! Two that cannot agree—one that cannot be severed. Our enemy is of our essence, taken from under our very heart. We are one by being two. We are unhappy both because we are two and quarrel, and because we are one and cannot part. Neither of us can go out of the other's hearing. We may cease to attend much to each other, but we are always within call. And every now and then, in the depth of our neglect, we are called, and we quail. And it is then that some men curse the voice they thought gone, and do the desperate things which outsiders think so inexplicable. Ah! people did not know what went on inside the spirit's house. They saw us walk out together, the two of us, us and our conscience, and we seemed on good terms with each other, seemed quite one. They heard nothing of the bitter quarrels indoors, the reproaches, the revilings, and the revilings again. But one day there is a crisis and a great to do. The man is gone, and his partner is not to be found. When they went they went together. We cannot get out of this critic's hearing, or leave our moral partner's presence. We are wedded under laws which allow of no divorce, for any incompatibility, cruelty or infidelity.

Who is this judge that follows us like our shadow? We did not appoint him. We did not give him his place. He is there in spite of us. He is no fiction of our imagination, else we would not be so afraid of him; we would not so dread our own creature. We fear him because he is in a position to threaten us or to ennoble us; because he does not suggest, but command. Temptation is only suggested, but duty is commanded. Sense solicits, but the soul enjoins. The place which we cannot help assigning to conscience (whether we admit it or not) is a place given it by another power than ourselves. But it is a power akin to us. It is our other. Conscience is something spiritual, a thinking being, a living moral mind.

And what follows from the fact that this spiritual "other" is our judge? Could any judge be a real judge who was not vested with power to enforce his threats and give his reward? Could one have the farce of a powerless judge in one's most serious affairs? It is impossible. This judge is one clothed with power; the judge of humankind must be invested with superhuman power to enforce the law he lays upon the human conscience. He must have all power—

for the command of duty is an absolute command. The judge must have absolute power. There must be no crevice of the universe into which the culprit could creep and reckon on escape. And for such a moral being who has all power over man we have but one name—God. Conscience is the Word of God within us; and moral responsibility means responsibility before God, the living God, and Christ, His living Grace.

For there is no possibility of going to the bottom of the matter and leaving out Jesus Christ. This error of so many thinkers is a historic evasion. Christ was and is the conscience of mankind and of God. He called Himself man's final judge. Was he deluded? He stands in the whole race as conscience does in each man. But He also means that the Eternal conscience is the Eternal love, that judgment is, in the heart of it, grace, that the judge is on our side and is our Redeemer. It is only love that can do justice, it is only grace that can right all wrong. The righteous Lord whom we cannot escape is our Saviour. Wrongs make far more sceptics than science; and the wrongs of history are being set right by a historic Redeemer. The moral malady of the race is mastered by the Saviour of the conscience. It is in history and in conscience that our hope lies. The conscience cries for forgiveness, and history brings to it the cross. There is the foundation of the soul and the security of the conscience, in the cross of history made ours in faith's experience of mercy. We must all come at last not to rational conviction but to this insight and venture of faith.

III

Life must be ethicised, all say; faith must do it, most say. But what is to ethicise faith, and especially Christian faith? The cross, must we not say? For can any faith be moralised except by its object? If there were a new religion it would have to grow out of the best religion we have—out of Christianity. And Christianity has grown out of the cross. The core of a new creed would be something still immanent not in the world but in the cross. Have we anything else for it but the cross and its cruciality (however newly read) as the re-creative centre of our moral world—the cross which is the central act of God's holiness, and the centre of the central moral personality, Christ? Solve Christ's cross and you solve all life. At that point concentrates what would be life's moral problem even if there were no God—supreme goodness and supreme calamity. But with a God it must be His goodness and His calamity there—unless He be impotent or indifferent. Which if He be not, then the presence of His goodness means the conquest of His calamity; which, again, could only mean the recovery of what He lost and whom He lost. There God's controversy with man draws to a head in the unity of reconciliation, which solves the tragedy of guilt and grief. There also we solve not only life but God. Whatever solves life solves God in the same act. Not indeed that it solves His constitution, but it solves His purpose. There the moral nature of God lives in the unity of an eternal redeeming act. "All's love and all's law"—there is but one spot in the world where that is entirely true; and the spot is Christ's atoning cross, the power centre of the moral world. And there, in that one eternal act of creative righteousness, is what gives unity to the life of all lives—the life of Jesus Himself. The Cross is central to Him who is the central moral figure of such a race.

Was the cross not central to Him? Where else shall we find the centre of that life? It must have one. Without a centre it would not be a unity. Its goodness would lie floating many a rood. And without a unity it would only be large in its notions but inadequate in power. Christ would be an ambitious ineffectual. Where in Him, then, does our faith find its unity? Where is the great meridian for reckoning a personality so vast? That unity could not lie loose and immanent in scattered words of spiritual wisdom, casual deeds of human kindness, or stray influences on certain souls. Is it in His character? It is impossible for us,

with all the insight of imagination, aided by all the resources
of scientific criticism, to trace in the character of Christ the
psychological unity which a modern taste demands. His
character is an infinite paradox, too large for our lens to
take in one picture. Besides, we are denied the data. For the
character of Christ was not the interest of the evangelists.
So the only unity we can find is not psychological—in the
tracing of motivation, for instance—which would be only
æsthetic; but it is moral, it is practical, it is in a thing done;
done with the total personality, and done once for all
between God and man. In a word, it is a theological unity.
It is the evangelical unity. There is no help for it. We must
go there at last, to the cross, where Jesus went before us.
Our thought must follow His feet, His conscience, His
obedience, the total *nisus* of His personality, to the cross.
The unity of His life was not in its cohesion but in its
consummation; not in its consistent symmetry, but in its
crucial effectual close, in the great, unique, and flowering
act of atonement. If His death was more than a martyrdom,
forming but the closing episode of His life (and if it was no
more, why do the Gospels give it such space and place?)
then it was atonement. In such a racial crisis we cannot dally
with the intermediate shades of possibility. Do not say it
was Reconciliation only. It was Atonement. For when a
relation like that of God and man is altered, it is altered on
both sides. And, besides, there can be no ultimate reconciliation of a race to a holy God without atonement. God's
moral order demands atonement wherever moral ideas are
taken with final seriousness; and man's conscience re-
echoes the demand. So much so that if men do not believe
that God atoned they will invent all kinds of cruel and
pagan devices to atone Him—just as we saw that men judge
Him if He do not judge them. But His own moral order and
moral nature demand an atonement. "The real and eternal
dignity of Humanity is so bound up with this cosmic order
of holiness that man would be diviner if he were broken
maintaining the honour of that holiness than if his mere

existence were secured by ignoring it." The New Testament at least cannot sever Atonement from Reconciliation. The greatest passage which says that God was in Christ reconciling says in the same breath that it was by Christ being made sin for us. The reconciliation is attached to Christ's death, and to that as an expiation. For reconciliation there means more than changing the temper of individuals; it means changing the relations between God and the race. It was a far mightier matter than subduing any mass of individuals. And it certainly drew on Christ at His centre. So, if the death of Christ was not a mere martyrdom on His life's extreme and negligible verge, when His best faculties were already spent and His best work behind Him, then it was the atonement at His life's true centre. His whole life was crowned here; it did not simply subside here in a dying fall. He came for the purpose of living His life a ransom. Was not His will to save one with His will to die? Or was the saving thing substantially done before He died? Was His death an otiose appendix? Was it not the revelation of His life's revelation, His life finding its object at last, His soul coming home to its own rest in the thing for which He was here? If we take care what we mean, it is more true to speak of the atoning life of Christ than of His atoning death. He is the atoning person, whose crisis, effect, and key is in His death. That act of His is the clue to all His action; because it was latent in it; for He was born as the result of a death He died in heavenly places before the foundation of the world (Philipp. ii. 1-12). His life of loving help to man was all produced under a divine "must" whose key is there. And His acts of blessing on earth produce a greater effect than they can by themselves explain. Behind everything He was and did here was the volume of a premundane volition (however unconsciously), as the geyser's force might be due to its source in a great and hidden lake high in inaccessible hills. The ground-tone of His soul throughout was less a humane sympathy than a divine obedience, an emptying of Himself at the Father's feet, of which His daily beneficence was but the passing expression. Just as all the transcendent acts that God does are but mere expressions of His one great immanent eternal act of love. Goodwin finely says: "As man, being sinful, sought out many inventions, so God, being loving, sought out a world of inventions to show His love." But the one eternal love that carries them all is in the brief and endless cross of Christ. His service of man was but index of His one perpetual and complete oblation to a holy God, His one continuous outpouring of His soul to death, consummated in suffering on the atoning cross. He Himself learned (if I may say so under the shelter of Hebrews) to construe all His life from the death whose divine necessity grew upon Him, and for whose accomplishment He was straitened in all else. In His death He Himself found Himself fully. And His expiring groan was also the relieved sigh of self-realisation. So that, if we are to choose the less of two errors, it is more true, with Paul, to let the life of Christ pale in the light of the cross than to let the cross and its atonement be lost behind His historical life.

Wherever we find the moral unity of Christ, there we find also the moral centre and the spiritual focus of the race whose spiritual representative He is. More and more we come to see that the centre of that supreme soul coincides with the central drama of man's whole historic conscience. And more and more (as I must go on to show) we are made to feel that the missing note in recent religion is just that keynote of judgment in His cross—judgment which, being twined with grace, makes the red thread both in the world's history and in the soul of Christ.

IV

2. To take the next line. It converges to the same point. There is no issue so vital to human society as righteousness. A society rises in the scale in proportion as righteousness is felt to be central and supreme. The right of the stronger may indeed be curbed by a social order which secures a

balance of interests; but a mere balance of interests is too mechanical to be the law of a society essentially moral; and as we ascend the scale we mark the growth of this one interest over all the rest—the ubiquity and prevalence of righteousness. It is the interest which is above all others humane and ethical. It deals with an ideal, and it makes it a reality for the conscience. And what it hears in the conscience is the social voice. Morality for the modern thinker is at least the total demand of the social will. It may be more, but it is that at least. It is a voice to the individual indeed, but a voice with a social word and a public note. The most hopeful thing in modern life is the growth of this ethical note, the progress of the passion for righteousness, and the elevation of the idea beyond individual integrity to social justice. The idea of righteousness carries us up from the mere man decent, through the upright man, to the truly social man; from the goodness of a man to the righteousness of a community; nay, beyond that, to a universal community thus just and right. But do we stop there? Surely all these still mean obedience to a law, a power, a standard, an authority. What of that power and authority itself? Where is the moral authority which is its own authority? Where is the goodness that is self-fed, self-ruled, self-moved, self-sufficing on an infinite scale? Where is the conscience that accounts for itself, and swears by itself because there is none greater? Are we not planted before the ineffable presence of one who is for ever fed from within with all the moral strength he needs, and is therefore the centre and foundation of the universe—the changeless, self-sustained, absolute, and *Holy* One? Is not the Holy God the heart of things and the head of things—the eternal good, central, self-poised, unmoved amid the millions of souls that lift to Him their eye, their need, their cry, their trust, or their hate, as His holiness goes out in love? Would entire faith be possible without that eternal and holy goodness, changeless behind all the love we trust? A love that could change we might love, but we could not trust it, however intense. It is the holiness within love that is the ground of such trust in it as makes religion. It is this holiness that enables us to meet the love of God with faith, and not merely with gladness; to trust it for ever, and not only welcome it at a time. And the Christian plea is that eternal holiness is nowhere secured and satisfied but in the sinless cross, which is therefore at the centre of life and things.

Our thought must take that line and that flight. In our pursuit of unity we expand from social justice to cosmic law, and pass from man's relation to man up to his relation to the universe; and so we are driven to its God. There may or there may not be other inhabited worlds than this, or other intelligences than man's; but surely the whole of God's righteousness is not exhausted in human justice. Were the whole race organised to the completest social justice and kindness, surely, till it was in due communion with His holiness, it would still be something less than the fulness of the whole counsel of the Universe. It would be unjust *to God* still. Unless, indeed, the race be the God. Unless our *Grand Etre* is Humanity, and there be no perfection beyond the unity of the race in love, order, and progress. But is there not a righteousness which is as much more than social as social is more than individual? The doctrine of the Trinity rose from the soul to say there is. Is there not a holiness as far above the stage of justice as justice is above integrity? Is cosmic not something wider even than social? And righteousness equally cosmic, social, and personal—what can it be but absolute holiness, righteousness as vast as a cosmos which science shows us to be infinite, and as social as the personal relations within a triune God?

This is a singular thing to me. We are in an age which teems with cosmic science, expands with cosmic ideals, and glows with cosmic emotion. That on the one hand. On the other hand, it is an age that thrills to the ethical ideal and the social passion of righteousness. How is it that for the holiness of a universal, triune, and therefore social, God there should be, even among the religious, so many that are either indifferent or shy? I have even found hostility. It is strange that there should be such *borné*, not to say vulgar, aversion for the theologian. He is simply an ethicist on a more than cosmic scale upon the authority of Christ. He is the rational expositor of a cosmic righteousness revealed as the infinite holiness. He faces, he inhabits, a world of moral realities whose action is perfectly sure and infrangible, which is not mocked, and whose laws in their kind are no more to be defied with impunity than those of Nature; for God spared not His own Son. That is the world of an absolute holiness. To the theologian the changeless holiness of God stands for the like capital to that which the physicist finds in the uniformity of nature. Press, therefore, the centrality of righteousness, and social righteousness, on the one hand. Rise to the cosmic range of thought on the other. The more you do both, as our age does, so much the more central for the cosmos, for universal existence, for all reality, must be the absolute righteous reality—*i.e.* the Holy God, the Holy Trinity; and the more stable and unsparing must be both His demand and His deed. These meet in the cross. If in His deed He spares not His own Son it is because the welfare of the universe is bound up, above all else, with the unsparing nature of His holy, loving law, whereof that willing Son is the historic witness, warranty, and "co-efficient Creator."

From another point of view, I do not find it quite easy to understand how it should be that many noble champions of a social righteousness can sit down under such an arrest of thought as they accept. Or it is an arrest of moral experience, all the more surprising in so much moral enthusiasm? Your passion for public righteousness or social justice (I would crave leave to say to them) you nourish as a universal ideal. And more. Your conflict is sustained by the vision of an ideal which is not merely æsthetic; that is, it is not duly met by your contemplation alone. But it is ethical and practical. It descends upon you with the force of a demand. Your moral ideal does not simply exist to be beautiful in some corner, or even in some central spot, like a marble dream in some *salon carré* of the world's Louvre. But it descends on you out of heaven from God, or what for you is God. It comes to you with no mere spectacular effect, but with compelling power. It lays its demand upon you to translate it into effect. It makes you not its amateurs but its organs and champions. It lies and presses upon your conscience, and not merely your imagination. But such an imagination of righteousness is not only so large as to be cosmic, nor only so weighty as to be exigent, but it is fine, piercing and pervasive in proportion. The breadth and the height and the depth of it are equal. The more lofty the righteousness is, and the more universal, so much the more subtle, searching, and exacting it must be. Can you have a telescopic infinity which is not microscopic as well? Can you think of a moral ideal for the whole world which is not urgent also on each whole soul? You feel the exigent, revolutionary demand of this general and eternal righteousness on society; you feel the mockery that current society offers to that ideal. How is it that, with your passion for moral thoroughness, it does not search and abash your own conscience more than appears? How, if it be so imperative for society, does it find so much that is impervious in you? (I speak but of what you allow to appear.) The society it tries to its base includes you as a moral monad. How are you so sceptical about its inquisition of you, so stoical in the self-respect of your apostolate, or so reticent about any humiliating or shattering visitations of you, however rare? Your apostolate of that unearthly righteousness is most convinced, sincere, and earnest. How do you escape the guilt, the fear, the repentance of it? Where has moral fear gone from the cultured world? Does the moral power only deal with social affairs, with a collective responsibility? How does your ethical sensibility react at wrongs but fail at sins? Have you none? Or no light that throws them up as sins, and burns and brands them into you? How is it that your indignation shows so little trace of reacting and deepening into humiliation? The parable you take up against society in the name of public righteousness, how is it that you are not driven to turn it upon yourself? (Do forgive me, but there is no discharge in this war, and men must press each other hard here.) Are you really able to face your own conscience, your own moral memory, with the same confidence as that with which you perhaps confront the egotists and capitalists who keep man from his social paradise? Does the moral analysis you apply to rend them never turn upon you with so much the more deadly subtlety as your standard is higher than theirs, and as you are better able to read yourself than them? How is it that the demand of entire social righteousness upon society fails to become the demand of complete, infinite holiness upon you? Is the moral world less than absolute and eternal— and penetrating, unsparing, accordingly? You are so worthily exigent, I do not understand why you are not more so; why, as you are so uncompromising, you are not more thorough; why your ethic is not co-extensive with your personality, why it is not a positive personal religion as it is a social theory for you; why, as you are undoubtedly modest, you have never gone on to humility; and why, with that modest sense of unworthiness, you do not feel yourself damnable, if only as a member of a solidary race which, if there be condemnation at all, is under a collective and conclusive condemnation.

Can it be that your moral standard, high and wide as it is, needs still to be truly universalised by theology of a practical kind? You have a high ideal, which you insist on laying upon all souls. Your motto is "Thorough." Do you not need (do forgive me if I am thorough too) one more high, more subtle, more comprehensive, more uncompromising, more holy, which will force its way into your whole soul, even to the rending of it, it may be? Your large moral world needs to rise heaven-ward in its ethical note till it break into a spiritual world whose height and depth and breadth are equal—a world as thorough in its spiritual penetration as it is in its moral exigence. Does your moral ideal pierce as much as it presses? Are its eyes as fiery as its wings? Would it not press much harder if it pierced much more? Does it search as powerfully as it urges? Has it power as it has weight and worth? Does your ideal of righteousness not need, ere it can master the soul, to become the ideal of a holiness before which you cannot stand? Is righteousness possible for society till holiness get its own?

You are too engrossed with the soul's conduct instead of the soul's quality. Your society would be but a mosaic of souls instead of a body of Christ. You would change men without changing the inmost heart, change conduct and relations without changing life. You would increase men's power of will without altering the style of will. But "the supreme ethic," says Weinel, "is not, like other ideals, beyond our power in its height, so much as it is beyond our own will in its nature." You are working on the level of the self-respecting moral gentleman, of the admirable English university product, who is in a position to live comfortably on his moral means, absorb spiritual ideas, and ignore spiritual powers as if they were no nearer than London neighbours. But the moral issue of the world is fought in a far more inward region than that, and turns on a far more inward crisis. "There are no *rentiers* in the moral life." And the battlefield of Christianity is not the clean and solvent soul of the moral *rentier*, the moral gentleman, but it is the moral bankrupt. There are far more of these than the refined English gentleman or lady knows, far more than writers on social subjects know, far more than is realised by those who handle the final moral issue with no other equipment than liberal thought and current culture. The moral crisis of society is in a region which you may know little of. You are bred, perhaps, in the sober, unbitten, and untragic atmosphere of intellectual West Ends, where evil is a study and not a curse. You have never felt the bottom drop out

of your own soul, the ground give way beneath your own
moral nature, while flying voices scream that Macbeth has
murdered sleep. You are masters of current ethic, but dilettanti of the moral soul. You have never had the experience
which would give you intimate knowledge of the life that
lies outside your ordered ways and kindly sets. You know
no more than to say that a tragic repentance is rare now
and the sense of sin being outgrown, or that there are
few people who live in actual personal relation with Jesus
Christ, or are governed by His will. Why, there is not a
section of the Church, and certainly of the Free Churches,
that could not show them in thousands. You have not
the experience of the priest in the confessional, or the
trusted pastor in his intercourse with his flock. I would
go a long way round to avoid offending you, but how
can any detour prevent me from saying that, high, wide,
and fine as your moral range is, you lack some experience
of men, and some moral sensibility at spiritual pitch? You
respond to a supreme good, but you do not to the Holy
of Holies. Your supreme good is but in the making. Your
righteousness far exceeds scribe or Pharisee, but you do
not rise to thorough self-judgment; nor from that to the
consciousness of the perfectly holy Self that judges even
your judgment of yourself. A few even outdo my audacity
with *you* in a kind of intellectual levity with *us*. They venture to lecture the theologians with an ill-veiled contempt
for their methods, if not always for their beliefs. They
lecture them both on their spirit and *their subject*, without
giving any indication that they have themselves studied.
in a scientific way, either a book of the New Testament
or a single metaphysical master, or a single theological
classic. Nay, they have been known to propound a theology
publicly, giving clear indication that to them epistemology
is a foreign country, moral philosophy an unknown region,
and ethical ideas quite tractable with a cosmic calculus.
But I willingly admit few have this confidence. And they
cannot well be treated on my present line. They treat the

problems of metaphysics with a mere hypo-physic, and wield a calculus of the subliminal more than the absolute, one more appropriate to the powers of a mystic, gnostic abyss than to the Eternal and Living God.

What lies incumbent on society to your mind (if I have your leave to return to you) is a law of righteousness. Yes, but what is it that lies incumbent, urgent, searching upon you for society, nay, for the sake of the power which is above society? Society is a collective and impersonal entity, and a law is all very well for that. But the soul is no mere impersonal entity. And the power that should rule it is no mere moral order, and no scheme of righteousness, and no Church, nor society. It must be another soul, the righteous source of rights and home of duties, self-sufficing in its righteousness, a soul absolutely holy, and holy unto infinite love. Would it not be possible to gain the whole world for righteousness and lose our own soul? If you say that that is absurd, that to lose the soul in such altruism is to find it, I recall that the supreme Teacher of that doctrine spoke only of losing the soul "for my sake and the gospel's," not for our neighbour's. And might I further remind you that, by the most enlightened and modern interpretation, that peril of a soul lost for public righteousness was the essence of the temptation of Christ Himself? His tremendous sense of moral power presented to Him the possibility of conquering a social righteousness in man for God on lines which ignored the holy will of God in the cross. What might He not have done for a reformed society, by a Cromwellian empire with an Ironside army, or by such service of man as made the regeneration of the mature Faust? But where would His own soul have been then, in the face of *His* calling of God, whose grace to Him was to make Him taste death for every man? There are things which we may not sacrifice to the most promising and beneficent of social causes. Neither men nor women may unsex their soul for any dream or phase of the Righteousness of God. But why should they not if social effect be all?

Over all your judgment of yourself or your society in

righteousness is the judgment of your righteousness by the holiness[1] of God. And practically that is the holiness of God in Christ. But you present me, perhaps, with two difficulties. First, that you find the divine love in the mind of the Christ of the Gospels, but not the divine holiness; for He does not speak of it. And second, that criticism has so reduced your data that it is very little we can say about the consciousness of Christ. But are we, then, come to this, that we cannot speak with any force of conviction about Christ as the first moral figure in history? You will not go so far as that, perhaps. But if He be the first, is Humanity such a poor thing, even its most eminent, that He has been unable to prevent His choicest followers for two thousand years from a moral blunder so great as that of finding in Him the very incarnation of the holiness of God, and in His cross its supreme and complete assertion? They have not preached Him as the world prophet of social righteousness; they have persisted in finding Him the incarnation of God's holiness; and they have made His effect on social righteousness to depend on that. Have they made a tremendous moral mistake? Was idolatry of Himself the chief legacy of our greatest man to posterity?

I have in my venturous mind not the popular religious dilettanti of a social reformation upon ethical lines, but earnest and accomplished students of that matter. And yet I must make bold to say, reluctantly and with great respect, that their obsession by the theological antipathy has made them such victims of theology (by its negation), and has so narrowed their mind thereby, that they have never taken due measure of Christ as a moral fact, still less as a moral factor in history. They have indeed been interested in the historical Christ, and they have owned the spell of His character in the procession of prophets. Carlyle did, for instance. But they have not dealt as seriously with the moral

[1] Perhaps I ought to have been explicit before now that by holiness is not meant anything so abstract or subjective as mystical absorption, but the whole concrete righteousness of existence, self-sustained at white heat. For our God is a consuming fire.

meaning of the fact as with its moral effect or its æsthetic or historical aspect. They have never integrated Him into the moral philosophy of history, into the spiritual organism of the race—as theology has at least tried to do. The historic or the ethical sense will carry a man far. But it will not carry him as far as the person of Christ takes him, if he give to that path a mind unstunted by scientific methods, or unstupefied by religious sentiment. You cannot treat Christ adequately by the historic sense, psychic research, cosmic emotion, the canons of natural ethic, or tender affection. The only adequate treatment of a fact so unique as Christ is the treatment proper to the moral nature of such a fact, the treatment it elicits and inspires, the treatment to which in the first disciples we owe anything that we know about Him, the treatment by faith. You must trust Him ere He seem worthy of your trust. He is really God only to the faith which has confessed Him as Saviour. His incarnation is an evangelical and not a logical demand. The Church's views about His person were forced upon those whom He not only impressed but regenerated, forced on them by the logic of living faith poring on the new creation that had passed them from death into life. It was only the scientific forms of these views that were affected by the philosophy of the hour, which did not, and cannot, give the certainty of their substance. It was a real redemption, making the Church's experienced life of faith, that Athanasius sought to express by the metaphysical Trinity. And the experienced verdict (and not merely the orthodox deposit) of His living Church in history is, that He is the incarnate holiness of the world and of Eternity; that Christ is no mere part of past history, but the soul of the race's total life; and no mere starting-point for the ideal, but the living object of each age's absolute faith. To trust Him is not a leap in the dark, but it is a venture none the less. It is a venture of courage and not of despair, of insight and not of bewilderment. In an age like this the greatest moral courage lies, not in challenging faith, as the crude public believes, which believes in little more than pluck. That is cheap heroism now. But true courage lies in pursuing, amid the dullness of the public, the desolations of criticism, the assaults of foes, and the treason of friends, such faith as still places the precious soul, the wondrous age, and the cosmic world for ever and ever in those hands which twenty centuries ago were nailed for our advantage to the bitter cross. To do that with open eyes to-day is a very great achievement of the soul, a very great venture of faith, and a very great exercise of moral courage of the silent and neglected sort. The world knows nothing of its debt to those who for the soul's sake are incessantly facing and laying the spectres of the mind.

V

3. If now we turn from the passion for unity, which carries us from a soul to a world, and from a world to the cosmic soul of God; if we further turn from the passion for universal righteousness, which carries us up to the supreme and holy judgment upon the cross; if we turn to the passion of human kindness, we are borne on, with the same high compulsion, to the Grace in the cross.

The effective sympathy of man for man has historically sprung from the grace and pity of God. I say the effective sympathy. The Stoics had a fine humanism which spread to include the whole race; but it was only in idea. It could not translate itself into action. Its finest representative was the severest of persecutors—I mean Marcus Aurelius. The real and active philanthropy of men has sprung from "the philanthropy of God." If you say it has taken long to grow, I remind you of the practical and popular benevolence of the first Christian centuries, and the silent beneficence and pity that make the sweetest note in the long history of the Church—so much of it unsweet. Appropriating, correcting, and hallowing the humanism of the eighteenth century by rooting it in God, this Christian humanism took, in the nineteenth, a new lease of life. And it has now come to a point of strain where it must draw deeply upon the inspirations of grace if it is to survive the disillusions that await a democracy merely human, and a socialism chiefly concerned with comfort. The rights of man are but revolutionary and sterile without the grace of God. As in France and America, they do not make brotherhood, so much as a negative, *borné* and prickly liberty. The love of man for man owes more to the grace of the cross than to any other influence. And no other influence can keep it alive or preserve it from futile sentiment. Those who see most of men, who have most intimately and practically to do with them, and who therefore see shrewdly into the average man, are not among the great lovers of men. Nor are we ourselves sometimes, when the strain of their contradiction grows tense, till we come out of the holy place where we met with God's love. When the capitalist stops his charities because his property is threatened by legislation we learn how short in the fibre is the charity which is not founded on the love and pity of God. The real test of the love of man does not come till we love our enemies. The love of our enemy is only the love of our neighbour true to itself through everything. For an employer to love the strikers that have ruined his business after a long and bitter war is not in nature. Yet that is the kind of tax to which the love of man is at last exposed. And there is only one source in the world to feed it and keep it alive—which is God's love of His bitter enemies, and His grace to them in repaying their wrong by Himself atoning for them on the cross. Central to all our humane kindness at last is the grace of the cross. The grand human strike against God would ruin both the workers and the Master did He not, in His love's tremendous resource, find means over their heads to save both His cause and theirs out of the wreck.

Human misery is too great for the human power of pity. No heart but that of holy God is equal to inviting into it all that labour and are heavy laden, to pitying on an adequate scale the awful tragedy of man or measuring man's suffering with that informed sympathy which is the condition of healing it. None can pity our human case to saving purpose but a God who treats it with more holy grace even than heart pity, and who is stronger to save our conscience even than He is quick to feel our wounds. Our suffering can only be finally dealt with by Him who is more concerned about our sin; who is strong enough to resist pity till grief has done its gracious work even in His Son; and who can endure not only to see the world's suffering go on for its moral ends, but to take its agony upon His own heart and feel it as even the victims do not, for the holy purpose, final blessing, and the far victory of His love. And this is what we have in the atoning cross of Christ. On the world scale we have it there alone. And the grace of the cross is as central to our human compassion as its judgment is to our public righteousness. The greatest human need is not only holy *love*, but *holy* love.

VI

This ethical, cosmic, eternal estimate of Christ cannot be based on His biography alone, or chiefly, but upon His cross, as we shall again find when we have surmounted the present fertile obsession by "the historical Jesus." Such an estimate is a judgment of value, a confession of faith, nay, a personal self-assignment. It is impossible to treat Christ adequately, except theologically and personally. Personally, for it is the theologian's hard and high fate to cast himself into the flame he tends, and be drawn into its consuming fire. And theologically, for we find the key of Christ's life in His work, find His work to be the cross, and find the cross to be God's atonement of Himself, His satisfaction of Himself and His reconciliation of the world, and especially of our own soul, once for all. The spiritual interpretation of Christ centres in the cross; and in the cross as a sacrifice offered *by* God more than *to* God, but to God more than to men. It is offered to the holiness of God before it is offered to the service of men. To both, indeed, but in that order. It is certainly not simply the classic case of man's service of man. That gives us a broad Christian but not a full Christ. And nothing but the fulness of Christ can replenish Churches emptied by mere orthodoxy or mere breadth. To banish the Atonement from the creative centre of Christianity is in the long-run so to attenuate Christ as to dismiss Him from Christianity, and condemn Him to be outgrown. As it was the cross that universalised Christianity, so also it is the cross that is the permanent and creative thing in it. All its faith, theology, and ethic are created and organised from the evangelical centre there. And this divine atonement to infinite holiness through loving judgment when its idea is truly ethicised is the only thing that can appeal at last to the heart of the modern passion for righteousness when it is thorough with itself, a passion which is so much more deep than its own consciousness goes. We avoid this centre only by our plentiful lack of moral wit, by the lack of evangelical experience, or intellectual thoroughness, or moral sequacity. Can we really think of righteousness without judgment, of a universal righteousness without a universal judgment—whether you put it in the pictorial shape of a last great assize or not? Must that judgment not arraign every soul? You cannot think (unless you fall to thinking of justice as mere utilitarian arrangement) of a universal righteousness which is not founded upon righteousness eternal and absolute, i.e. upon divine holiness. Can you think, then, of universal judgment except as the relation to that holiness of every soul? And not only of every soul, but of the whole soul ranged before the whole God and the holy God? Could a personal soul be judged by a mere historic process? Does it not call for a personal God? And if there be any religious protagonist of the sinful race—I own I tax you, and I am sorry, but it has taxed me more—must he not stand vicariously before the judgment of that God, and take home that Love under the moral conditions of a righteousness so universal, a holiness so absolute, and a sin so grave? This is what (in the Church's faith) Christ did, and did once for all. It is the supreme service He rendered to social righteousness, and consequently to eternal—if we could but for an hour get far enough away from social problems to take their measure and proportion, feel their foregone solution, and so find rest and power for our souls. He put His corporate race in right relation to a Holy God.

All this lifts Christ far above the level of a historic figure. A mere historic, stationary Christ is but a transitory Christ—which is a paradox. But you cannot tell the truth about the cross without a lie of the paradox. A Christ who stood fixed only at a point in history would be, by His very fixture, a transitory Christ, because but a temporary; because He would be outgrown and passed by the moving race. A Christ merely ideal, stationed at a fixed point on earth but magnified to an ideal upon the clouds, would become a *Brockengespenst*. He would be a mirage whose very grandeur and purity would shame us far more than help us. And He would shimmer before us like an aurora, when we needed to be warmed and reared by a perennial sun.

The new passion for righteousness, then, must end upward in a new sense of judgment; and especially among the religious, if their ethic is to grow more delicate and penetrating as well as more urgent. Social righteousness, unaccompanied by moral delicacy, inner penetration, and self judgment, could easily become another phase of Pharisaism. Love without holiness lends itself but too easily to dissimulation, to unreality. But to give God's judgment its due place in public righteousness is to raise ethic to religion, righteousness to holiness, and to make some kind of atonement inseparable from real faith on any social scale; and certainly on the social scale of a Church transcending and outstaying all the societies of men.

What is our social ardour to live on after a few disillusioning generations? What moral reserve are we providing for the vicissitudes of the great business of history?

IV

WHAT IS MEANT BY THE BLOOD
OF CHRIST?

IT is a question which is often asked how a phrase like "the blood of Christ" could be presented in such ethical terms as appeal to an age like our own. May I suggest the lines of a reply?

I

It would not have mattered a whit if no drop of blood had been spilt, if Jesus had come to His end by the hemlock or by the gallows. The imagery under which we speak of the situation would have been changed—that is all.

II

Nor would it have mattered if, instead of losing but some of His blood, He had bled to death. Whether no blood was shed, or every drop, was immaterial. That could only concern us if the virtue was in the blood as a substance, as it might be kept and applied in a reliquary. Had that been so, the sacrifice would not have been complete if a drop had remained in the body; while (on the same supposition) if not a drop had been shed there would have been no sacrifice at all.

There is, indeed, very little about the theory of the matter in the Old Testament. "Theories as to the meaning of ritual," says Dr. Bennett, "only arise after the origin of the rite has been forgotten." The chief hint is in Leviticus xvii. 11, as we shall see. But nowhere in the Old Testament does the value of the sacrificial blood lie in the blood itself. Nor does it lie in the suffering that might go with bloodshed. Nor does the final value lie even in the life symbolised by the blood, rich as we shall see that idea to be. We go behind

and above even that to the obedience of faith answering
God's will of grace. The value of the sacrificial rite lay
wholly in the fact of its being God's will, God's appoint-
ment, what God ordained as the machinery of His grace
for national purposes. Let it not be forgotten that in the
Old Testament what confronts God is the people much
more than the soul. It is of grace that He consents to receive
the proffered life and reckon the gift for public righteousness. In the Old Testament the acceptance is acceptilation.

III

On the other hand, blood or none, it would have mattered
a whole world if Jesus had met His death naturally, by
accident or disease. Everything turns, not on His life having
been taken from Him, but on its having been laid down.
Everything, for His purpose, turns on the will to die. But,
none the less, for that purpose, it had to be a death of moral
violence (inflicted, that is, by human wickedness and the
wresting of the law), to give its full force to both man's sin
and Christ's blood. "Men of blood," in the Old Testament,
were not mere killers but murderers. So that we say it
would have mattered a whole world if the death had not
been violent and wicked, if Jesus had died of disease in
His bed, or by accidental poison.

IV

It follows that the acceptable and valuable thing to God
was not mere demise, in whatever form. The Lord and
Giver of life can have no pleasure in life's extinction. The
death, even of Christ, could not have had divine value if
it had meant any acceptance of even a martyr death which
involved extinction and the dissolution of His personality.
His death was precious in God's sight as the conquest of
death, as the negation of death, as the ironic antithesis of
death, the surmounting of its accepted arrest, the capture
of its captivity. It is death as transition, not exinction; yet
it is transition not as mere metamorphosis, that is, not as a

mere step in a large *process*, not as a new stage of even moral growth, not as a fresh stadium in the normal evolution of a personality. There is involved in it a *crisis*. Take the case of resurrection. We do not get the full import of the idea of the resurrection if we see in it only a survival of personality, any more than if we treat it as a mere reanimation. Neither vital resuscitation nor mere personal persistence does justice to Christ's resurrection. It crowns a real moral crisis and achievement. It seals a decisive moral act. His death and resurrection really form two sides of one act. Christ's resurrection is but the obverse of the real personal crisis in His death. And His death is redemptive only as a personal moral deed. It is a moral conquest only as it is a crucial moral achievement, in which His personality was not only unscathed but consummated; and not only consummated but effectual, victorious, and decisive. The shedding of blood means this finality. It means something which touches the seat of life—as we might now say, puncture of the heart. It means the total surrender of a personality from its centre by the one means wherein personality both receives effect and produces effect—by means of a personal *act* of conquest which requires (but also releases) the whole resources of the personality. What God seeks is not a religious tribute or present, costly but partial; His self-complete holiness requires, to meet and satisfy it, a total holy self, in a real act or deed of gift once for all, the absorption and oblation of the whole self in a crucial and objective achievement. The essential thing was not self-sacrifice (which might be wilful, and often is wilful, as well as futile, or even mischievous), but sacrifice of the central self—not sacrifice *by* self but *of* self, and of the whole self; sacrifice not merely voluntary but personal, loving, and entire. Not till then is it striving unto blood. And we end by noticing that the offering of self here was the offering of a holy self to a holy God from sin's side; and that sacrifice, therefore, involved, in some form, the idea not only of substitution but of judgment. What Nathan (so early) required from

David in God's name was not only repentance and confession but satisfaction (2 Samuel xvii, 7, 13, 14).

I should like to go into more detail on these heads.

V

Jesus appeared among a people whose mode of execution was not as it is with us, but either by stoning or crucifixion. That is to say, it was with effusion of blood. That in the first place. In the second place, He appeared in an age and stage when the effusion of blood formed part of the religious ritual also—and indeed its central rite. In this external respect the criminal and the religious procedure concurred as they now do not. And, in the third place, for the great majority of the worshippers in Christ's day, the origin of the rite was quite forgotten; its genius, therefore, was ill-understood; and, accordingly, serious people had inevitably begun speculating, and framing theories of it, which Christianity took up, corrected, and enriched. By almost all Judaism the rite was taken as an *opus operatum*, as if the blood in itself had an atoning value or, at least, as if the performance of the bloody rite had this value, and had it as mere compliance with a divine regulation instead of congenial answer to a divine gift. The symbolic significance had gone. The why of the prescription did not trouble the general mind, though it did occupy the theologians of the day. The New Testament writers, therefore, whose whole spiritual world was now lit up and reorganised by the regeneration of the cross, had to take the current rite and the current language, and to restore to both the profound, moral, and spiritual religion of the Old Testament. We have still to do the same. We have still to treat in this way many of our own ancient ideas and terms, in spite of shallow and scrupulist protests from intellectualists rigidly righteous against playing with words or paltering with them in a double sense.

VI

There is nothing that is more necessary to note in regard even to the Old Testament sacrifice, there is nothing that more differentiates it from all pagan sacrifice, than the two truths, one speculative and one positive, set out in Leviticus xvii. 11. "The life of the flesh is in the blood: and *I have given it to you* upon the altar to make atonement for your souls: for it is the blood that maketh atonement by reason of the life." The two truths fundamental to the revealed (as distinct from the popular and pagan) idea of sacrifice are, therefore, these.

(1) The positive truth is that the sacrifice is the result of God's grace and not its cause. It is given *by* God before it is given *to* Him. The real ground of any atonement is not in God's wrath but God's grace. There can be no talk of propitiation in the sense of mollification, or of purchasing God's grace, in any religion founded on the Bible.

(2) The speculative and explanatory truth is that the pleasing thing to God, and the effective element in the matter, is not death but life. The blood was shed with the direct object, not of killing the animal, but of detaching and releasing the life, isolating it, as it were, from the material base of body and flesh, and presenting it in this refined state to God. (We allow, of course, for the current belief, in whose language the cultus was cast, that the blood was the seat of the life as no other element of the body was.) The creature had not to suffer. And it had to die only incidentally, in the course of getting away the life for a blessed purpose of God with man. The shedding of blood was certainly not a wreaking of punishment indifferently on guilty or innocent. This idea is quite foreign to the Bible. No fair critic of Christianity ought to regard it, and no informed one does. To urge it is only a piece of the intellectual levity and jaunty ignorance that so often go with much aggressive criticism, especially of the popular kind. In the Old Testament, moreover, the slaying of the creature was not intended to free the offerer from the death penalty;

because for the great sins that meant death and exclusion from the community there was no sacrifice. Instead, therefore, of being a gross conception, the Jewish use and speech of blood in this connection was a refinement on all other ritual—if we will but read with the historical sense. The flesh was eaten when drained of the blood; the blood could never be thus consumed. It was too sacred.

VII

We go a step farther in reading the Levitical praxis when we note that the material sacrifice was, and was meant to be, but an outward symbol of the real inner sacrifice, which was the offerer's self-oblation. The victim, or the gift, signified the inward and hearty submission of the donor to God's prior gift and provision. It was the living symbol of a life, *i.e.* of an obedient will. Man's gift to God was an individual appropriation of God's public gift to man in the provided way of access. The sacrifice as a mere tribute was worthless, a mere tax paid by unwilling fear. It must come freely. It must be the symbol and sacrament of the worshipper's self-surrender to God's positive will in the sacrificial act. Indeed, even when freely given, it was but a response, it was not absolutely spontaneous. It was not the worshipper's invention; it was God's prescription; the initiative was His. It was not a gift to God, but an appropriation of God's gift in the institution itself. All religion exists only as some kind of response to some kind of revelation. It is not fantastic ingenuity nor arbitrary originality. Man is most original in his religion; and yet his religion is the least original thing he has.

It is a very crude kind of scepticism now which regards the claim of divine authority for the Levitical system as a priestly fraud. It was part expression of an elect *nation*, whose inspiration took form in institutions as well as prophets. And the prophets who denounced sacrifice did so only when it was made an *opus operatum* and the ritual became a religion in itself. They were as one-sided, and yet as historically necessary, as our own Puritans, like Milton, who for the hour could only cope with Rome by denouncing ideas so truly divine (when not monopolist) as those of a liturgy or an episcopate.

Thus we have two things. The worship was ethical in its nature. And it was responsive and obedient in its form. The ritual act was valuable only as the organ of the ethical obedience. The sacrifices were consecrated by self-sacrifice. It was the offerer's will that lay on the altar. What was precious was not the thing, not the elements, but the act. It is thus that Protestantism truly construes each of its sacraments. The elements matter little, or their state. Fruit or water would do as well. The essential thing is the communal act, the act of communal obedience, in which the priest is the organ of a community priestly without him, and he is but the channel of God. The whole Hebrew system strove to keep down the place and value of the gift, and to worship, in spirit (i.e. *in actu*) and in truth, a seeking, acting, and giving God. Hecatombs were unknown. A widow's mite could be more sacramental than a nation's mint. The act was the precious thing. And the act treated not as a mere individual function, but as a deliberate exercise of will and self-disposal within a divinely instituted community—an act always responding in moral kind to the act of God's corporate will and grace which ordained it. It is God that makes religion and not man. Faith itself is the gift of God, being the echo of the Christ He gave to our race, and to each man only as a member of that race so redeemed. We are saved only on God's terms of a social redemption. Every man is saved only by the act which saved man.

VIII

What is offered up, therefore, is life in its most intimate, spiritual, and moral form. This does away with several unhappy notions. It does away with the notion that the pleasing, satisfying, atoning thing to God is suffering. It destroys the idea of Atonement as consisting in equivalent pain; as if the work of Christ was to suffer in a short time, by His divine intensity of being, the pains of the endless hell which we had earned. Suffering becomes a mere condition, and not a *factor*, in the sacrificial act. And then, as we have just seen, we get rid of the idea that the essence of the sacrifice, the *donum*, was any *thing*, any piece of property. It must be life. Blood means essential, central, personal moral life. Human sacrifice was so far right. Debased and dreadful, it yet had an instinct of right. Where it was wrong was in the concomitant idea that any person could have property in another person—as slave, child, or wife. The wrong idea was not that life was the sacrifice, but that a man could have any such property in souls as he could dispose of even for sacrifice, that he had sacrificial property in them, that he could do with them what he could really only do with himself, and not with himself even by way of mere immolation or suicide. The tacit and false assumptions in such immolation were (1) that souls could be the offerer's property (and therefore religious means instead of ends), and (2) that the highest sacrifice was a payment of property, even property so prized as human chattels. It was true that sacrifice by blood meant sacrifice of precious life. But our will is our dearest life, the thing we cling to most and give up last. Our will alone is our ownest own, the only dear thing we can and ought really to sacrifice. The blood as life means the central will, the self-will, the whole will, in loving oblation. This is the sacrifice even in God. The cross does not in the New Testament exhibit God as accepting sacrifice so much as making it. And it is never in the New Testament represented as the extremity of suffering, but as the superlative of death; it is not the depth of agony but the height of surrender; and that again is represented as the triumph of eternal life. It is the absolute active death of self-will *into* the holy will of God; but also *by* that will; the complete, central, vital obedience of the holy to the holy in a necessary act on the Eternal scale. A necessary act. It was in an act, and not in a mere mood of resignation. And in an act not gratuitously done (however voluntarily), not blindly done just to get some outlet for an irresistible instinct of self-sacrifice. It was an act made necessary by the organic pragmatism and moral unity of Christ's whole life; which was a whole life rooted in the organic context and moral necessity of a national history; which history again was integrated into the spiritual necessity of God's holy purpose for the whole race and its redemption. Christ must die not simply of the blindness and blunders of men, but because by God's will He was the incarnation of that holiness which, as it moves through history, necessarily makes sin so sinful and wickedness so furiously to rage. The *must* was not merely in the Jewish nature, but in the nature of holiness, as soon as it came to close quarters with human sin. The real nature of the Incarnation lies in what might (with some violence perhaps) be called the moral polarity, the reciprocal identity, of Christ's holiness with the holiness of God. The holy God alone could answer Himself and meet the demand of His own holiness. So Paul felt in his own relation to Christ's holiness. "Not I, but Christ living in me."

We make sacrifices, and costly ones, which yet do not draw blood from us. They do not come home. They do not go to the very centre of our life. They do not touch the nerve or strain the heart. A man may devote the toil of a self-denying life to a book of stupendous research on the gravest subjects, which yet makes no call on his inmost self, and is not written with his blood but only with a sweating brow. We get the toiler in calm research, the genius of scholarly combination perhaps, but not the man. But when we speak of the blood of Christ we mean that what He did drew upon the very citadel of His personality and involved His total self. The foundations of His great deep were broken up. His whole personality was put into His work and identified with it; not merely His whole interest or ambition. The saving work of God drew blood from Christ as it drew Christ from God—and not from God's side only but from His heart. Christ's work touched the quick of

God; as it touched the quick also of His own divinest life, and stirred up all that was within Him to bless and magnify God's holy name. He poured out His soul unto death. God, in His insatiable holy love, was exigent even on Him, and spared not His own Son. Man's sin drew upon all God's Son, and taxed the Holiest to the height. It made call upon what is most deep in Christ and dear to God— Himself, His person, His vital soul, His blood. The love of God is only shed into our hearts in the shedding of that most precious blood.

IX

We have risen to a stage when sacrifice, in the ritual sense, in the sanguinary sense, has long had no real place in our religion or worship. The language of sacrifice, therefore, has no meaning for us, except as it covers acts or requirements which are at heart ethical. But in passing to this stage we are not simply repudiating Hebraism. We are interpreting it. We are not casting its old clothes. We are liberating the moral soul of Hebraism. We can now treat history far more sympathetically than Carlyle did. We are setting free the idea it carries, and disengaging its true genius. We are not making a construction. We are not reading a later thing into Hebraism. We are seizing on an element which the great Hebraism always had at its core and foundation, and which only the popular religion and its debasements submerged,[1]—the element of initial and proffering grace on the one hand, and of obedience answering by faith's self-offering on the other. God made the first sacrifice, to which all man's sacrifices are but response. Our best is but the faint echo of His. And we can never come to a depth of sacrifice where God has not been before us and outdone us. If we make our bed in hell He is there.

[1] The whole secret of treating the Old Testament is the art of disentangling the divine revelation from the popular religion, even within the prophet's own mind, and marking how the one gradually emerged through the other, and shed its shell. There are many fragments of the shell still adhering, even in the revelation of the New Testament, which it is the business of modern criticism to detach.

This is the meeting-point of the priestly and prophetic streams in the Old Testament. To obey everywhere is better than sacrifice. The good priest would have said that as honestly as the good prophet. For the ritual was but an act of obedience. That was its real worth. It was only hearty obedience, and not mere compliance, that gave sacrifice any divine value, and raised it above being a mere subsidy from us, or a mere exaction by God. The sin-offering becomes in its nature a thank-offering. It was a case of ethical obedience with the true priest no less than with the true prophet. It was the surrender of the will. Only in the one case it took the form of worship and in the other of conduct. And for life the one is quite as needful as the other. The obedience of the whole man and the fulness of his life demand both, especially on a national scale—but each has its own place, and neither can be substituted for the other. Thus Christ consummated the priest no less than the prophet of the sacred community. It is one-sided to see in Him only the victory of the prophetic line. His offering of Himself was the eternal Spirit of His people's past, returning, in complete satisfaction, to God who gave it.

X

While we can never cease to speak or think of the blood of Christ we must take much pains to interpret its true idea to our modern conditions. If we speak of the sacrifice of Christ we must construe it in the ethical terms presented by its own dominant holiness and demanded by the modern passion for righteousness; and we must for this end avoid such a use of imagery as discourages that effort—like the first verse of Cowper's fine hymn, "There is a fountain filled with blood." It is not a mere matter of taste that moves our protest against it.

But do we succeed in this attempt to ethicise when we regard the death, or the cross, of Christ as the supreme glorification of heroic self-sacrifice, moving, and exalting, and purifying us, as the genius of tragedy is? Or do we succeed even when we regard the cross simply as the *manifestation*, the great object-lesson to us, of God's love under the arduous conditions of sacrifice? Or do we succeed when we regard its first and sole object as being to move mankind to repentance, and thus to supply the condition of forgiveness, instead of being itself God's act of forgiveness? Is there anything conveyed by the extreme phrase "the blood of Christ" which is not conveyed by the idea of sacrifice, or the idea of revelation, or the idea of a *Büsspredigt?* Yes. There is one whole side—the side indicated by the words, judgment, expiation, or atonement; the side which, ever since Anselm, has magnified the weight and sinfulness of sin, as the sense of God's holiness rose. And this is a side which it is absolutely impossible to drop from Christianity without giving the Gospel quite away in due time. Individuals, of course, can remain Christian while they discard it, but the Church cannot.

We may and we do show love, pity, and kindness to those around us with a divine ingenuity and assiduity. But that is not redeeming love. The genius of all philanthropy is not redemption but amelioration. Charity does not reconcile; only justice does—as the bitter spirit of rebellion at the end of the age of philanthropy shows. It has not the element of sin, righteousness, judgment, and new creation. It is not the holy, searching, sanctifying love which made the cross of Christ. It has not the ethical note of judgment. Indeed, there is no weaker feature in much current kindness of affection than its impatience of judgment, of real criticism, and its lack of courage to bear, or to exercise, it in a helpful and saving way. Very few, for instance, of those who love the people nor would see them wronged, love in such a way as implies courage to tell their clients to their face of the things in them which are more fatal to their progress than all disabilities. And the deadly effects of parental weakness in this way have long formed a moral commonplace—now more common and more in place than ever.

The appetite for praise is much more keen than for perfection (which is another name for holiness, Matt. v. 48), and love doubts love which ventures on rebuke. So religion takes, in this respect, the colour of the time; and in preaching a love without judgment it swamps conscience in heart, and laps the sin in a warm mist of kindness for the sinner. Much more is here involved than any orthodoxy. One only cares to deal with a false theology because it is the fatal source of false religion, false ethic, and a false public note. And a true theology is of such moment because it embodies those ethical powers and acts which sit at the centre of human life and mould the whole course of human history to its destiny. A true theology is the moral philosophy of the Eternal, the ethic of the Eternal; and at the present bewildered hour it is more needed than religion, for the sake of religion. What religion needs most of all is to regain the moral salt of judgment.

XI

When we speak of the blood of Christ, then, we mean that what He did involved not simply the *effort* of His whole self (as it might be with any hero taxed to his utmost), but the *exhaustive obedience and surrender* of His total self. But, on the line of judgment just named, we have to go farther, in a direction indicated in a passing way already (p. 92). We have to say that it involved obedience of no gratuitous and arbitrary kind, no "voluntary humility," no self-willed, self-chosen obedience, no self-created task, as the manner of some great devotees is; but it obeyed the necessity of an actual historic and spiritual situation. It represents no mere historic necessity, rising from Christ's relation to Israel and its past. But there is a divine must which Israel's history itself was set to serve and failed. It was complete obedience on a universal scale to the moral requirements of grace, *i.e.* to a holy grace, to what the holiness of grace required in a situation of racial sin. The sacrifice of Christ was inevitable by His holiness in such a world. Holiness must suffer in the midst of sin. And it was a sacrifice made to the Holy. It was not offered *to* man but *for* man, even when we magnify to the utmost its immense effect *on* man. It was first offered to holy God, to hallow His name and make it honourable.

But in saying this what do we say? We have passed upward from the idea of *sacrifice* to the graver and more ethical idea of *judgment*. We recall the fact that the effusion of blood was a mark not merely of temple ritual but of criminal execution. It was involved not merely in the cultus but in the civil code and social order based on God's righteousness. And full self-sacrifice to a holy God involves by analogy the submission of self to the moral order and judgment of God. Holiness and judgment are for ever inseparable. To ignore them or to sever them is the central failure of theological liberalism. The note of judgment runs through the whole genius of Israel's history as surely as do sanctity, submission, salvation and the Kingdom—and especially on its prophetic prophetic side. God must either punish sin or expiate it, for the sake of His infrangibly holy nature. Do let us take the holiness of God centrally and seriously, not as an attribute isolated and magnified, but as God's very essence and nature, changeless and inexorable. The holiness of God is a deeper revelation in the cross than His love; for it is what gives His love divine value. And it is meaningless without judgment. The one thing He could not do was simply to wipe the slate and write off the loss. He must either inflict punishment or assume it. And He chose the latter course, as honouring the law while saving the guilty. He took His own judgment. It was a course that produced more than all the effect of punishment, and in a better, holier way. It was vindicative and not vindictive. It re-established the holiness; it did not just confound the sinner. Expiation, therefore, is the very opposite of exacting punishment; it is assuming it. Nor is it exacting the last farthing in any quantitative sense. That is not required in a full, true, and sufficient satisfaction. The holy law is satisfied by an adequacy short of equivalency, by due confession of it and not by exaction; by due confession which fully gauges the whole moral situation, as neither sin nor love alone could do; by practical confession in an experience as holy to God as it was sympathetic to man; and by practical confession of God's holiness far more than man's guilt.[1] What a holy God requires is the due confession of His holiness before even the confession of sin.

And this is the only sense in which Christ could confess from His inmost experience, could confess with His blood. His practical and entire confession of holiness from the midst of the sinners He loved is the divine significance of His blood. No obedience to a holy God is complete which does not recognise His judgment, and recognise it in the practical way of action, by accepting it—not necessarily in amount but in principle; not equivalently, as to amount of suffering, but adequately, as to confession of sanctity; and it confesses it practically, silently, in act and suffering. And who but God could adequately confess in action the holiness of God? And who but the sinless could confess the sin of man? Who else but the holy could realise what it meant as sin?

Love in sacrifice means pain. But for holy love it means moral pain. And moral pain is something more than passive; it is active. It is not the pain of a sting merely, but of wrath; the pain not of a wrong but of rectifying it; not of grief but of judgment. Holiness must in very love set judgment in the earth. We have here to do, then, especially with the order of pain that sin gives to God, in reacting against it, in judging and destroying it. The blood of Christ stands not simply for the sting of sin on God but the scourge of God on sin, not simply for God's sorrow over sin but for God's wrath on sin. It expresses not simply the bleeding of the feet that seek the sinner but the bloodshed of the battle that

[1] Here McLeod Campbell and Moberly seem to me to come short. They do not get their eye sufficiently away from the confession of sin.

destroys the prince of this world, that breaks in us the guilty entail, and establishes the holy kingdom. The total self-oblation of man to God means before all else that dread recognition of holiness which from sin's side must be felt as God's wrath and curse; its recognition in experience as judgment; and its recognition on a scale adequate to both God and man in their greatness. The prime question of religion is not how shall I feel a child of the Father, but how shall I stand before my judge, how shall man be just with God? What must I do to be saved? Christ's first business in saving was to honour the Father's holy love. He saved man because He first saved God from being mocked by man. His submission to judgment was not simply His experience of doom and suffering as incidents of life, but His submission to them as God's purpose for Him, and His confession of them as expressions of the holiness of God and of His power to make man's wrath praise Him. It was not merely a collision with historic forces and social powers in Israel, but the recognition, within these, of the holy wrath of God. It was the power so to deal with man's wrath against God as to accept God's wrath against man, and make sin farther the purpose it seemed to foil. The necessity of Christ's death was created more deeply by God's holiness in Him than by the perversity of the men it exasperated. No one could reveal a holy God by any amount of suffering or sacrifice which did not recognise this element of judgment,—did not atone. *No real revelation is possible except as Atonement and Redemption.* I do not mean that Atonement came as a preliminary to clear the ground for the revelation, but that the revelation came and could come only in the form of Atonement.

It is this element of judgment, of Atonement, of dealing with a doom, not to say a curse, that is conserved in the historic and symbolic word blood. It transcends the ritual idea of self-sacrifice not only by indicating the absoluteness and inwardness of it, but by keeping to the front the civil and social idea of judgment. It is not death that atones, but that supreme act and expression of holy, obedient life which does such justice to God's holiness as the Son alone could do; and which is possible only under the conditions of death, and of such death as Christ died. The death of Christ was an experience in His life, yet it was always the dominant, and at last the crowning one, which gave meaning to all the rest even for Himself—as He came to learn. It was a function of His total life, that function of it which at once faced and effected the saving, the last, judgment of God. His blood was shed in Gethsemane as truly as on Calvary; but it was on Calvary that it rose to seal all and to found for ever our peace with God. It was there that it rose to establish our evangelical faith in us, to establish it not as an affection simply but as life-confidence and self-disposal, as a faith that turns not upon the filling of the hungry heart but upon the stilling of the roused conscience both in God and man by a complete satisfaction and forgiveness once for all.

XII

We associate blood with ultra-realism. A morbid phase of the tendency is found in the crowds that gather to see the stain of an accident, still more of a murder. That is a case where the blood is treated as a thing, for its own sake, and not significantly as a symbol. But as a symbol it stands for moral realism the most poignant, and central, and eternal. In our religion it means that Christ touches us more nearly and deeply than our pain does, or our guilt. What in us harrows the heart in Him harrowed hell. "Hell from beneath is moved for Thee to meet Thee at Thy coming." He revolutionises the eternal foundations of our moral world. But it means also that He came from a region in the moral reality of God deeper than sin or grief could shake. It signifies the very heart and Godhead of God, the holy reality of God, an eternal act of the whole God, one drawing on the whole Trinity, therefore a final act in the heavenliest places in Christ. In being "made sin," treated as sin (though not as a sinner), Christ experienced sin as God does, while he experienced its effects as man does. He felt sin with God, and sin's judgment with men. He realised, as God, how real sin was, how radical, how malignant, how deadly to the Holy One's very being. When Christ died at sin's hands it meant that sin was death to the holiness of God, and both could not live in the same world. When He rose it meant that what was to live and rule in the world was the holy God. Dying as man, Christ placed His whole self beside man under the judgment of God. He was beside man in court but on God's side in the issue, confessing God's holiness in the judgment, and justifying His treatment of sin. Justifying God! A missionary to the North American Indians records that having seen his wife and children killed before his eyes, and being himself harried in bonds across the prairie amid his tormentors, he "justified God in this thing." I do not know a sublimer order of experience than from the heart to bless and praise a good and holy God in despairs like these. It is to this order of experience that the work, the blood, of Christ belongs. And there is no justification of men except by this justification, this self-justification, of God. Never is man so just with God as when his broken, holy heart calls just the judgment of God which he feels but has not himself earned; and never could man be just with God but through God's justification of Himself in the blood of Christ.

We cannot in any theology which is duly ethicised dispense with the word satisfaction. It was of course not a quantitative replacement of anything God had lost, nor was it the glutting of a God's anger by an equivalent suffering on who cares whom. It was no satisfaction of a *jus talionis*. But it was the adequate confession, in act and suffering, "Thou art holy as Thou judgest." That man should confess this vicariously and victoriously in Christ crucified and risen is the re-establishment of God's holiness in the world. We can only understand any justification of man as it is grounded in this justification—this self-justifica-

THE BLOOD OF CHRIST

tion—of God. The sinner could only be saved by something
that thus damned the sin. The Saviour was not punished,
but He took the penalty of sin, the chastisement of our
peace. It was in no sense as if *He felt* chastised or condemned
(as even Calvin said), but because He willingly bowed,
with a moral understanding possible only to the sinless,
under the divine ordinance of a suffering death and judgment which was holily ordained to wait on the sin of His
kin. The blood of Christ cleanseth from *all* sin. The metaphor denotes the radicality, totality, and finality of the
whole action in the realism of the moral world—which
even high sacrifice, not resisting unto blood, only slurs or
shelves—when it does not toy with it.

It is notable that Christ speaks of His blood only at His
life's end, while during life He spoke only of forgiving
grace without any such expiation (except in the ransom
passage). Why was this so? Was it not, first, because His
grand total witness, which death but pointed, was to the
grace of God's holy love; and the exposure of sin could only
come by the light of that revelation? And was it not, second,
because His revelation and offer of holy grace without
sacrifice and judgment failed of its effect; because even the
great, uplifted, and joyful *invitation*, "Come unto Me," failed
till it was *enacted* from the mighty gloom of the cross; because
only the uplifting of the cross, and not the uplifting of His
voice, draws all men unto Him; because in Christ mere
prophetism, stern or tender, found its greatest failure;
because, as prophet, He could neither make His own cleave
to Him, nor make the people see how much more than
prophet He was; He could not keep them from murdering
their Messiah? But, according to Old Testament ideas,
this murder was the consummation of high-handed sin, of
the kind of sin that had no expiation, that was unprovided
for in the Hebrew economy of grace. There was no grace
for the deliberate rejection of grace. There a new expiation
must come in, that would cover even this. The death of
Christ expiated even the inexplicable sin that slew Him,

and the sin of a whole Humanity whose religious protagonist Israel was.

XIII

Does it not follow that, when we use such a word as "satisfaction" in connection with the blood of Christ, we do not think of meeting with compensation a mere law formulated or formulable, however holy—far less a divine fury; but of meeting, confessing, justifying a God of holy love with a love equally holy from the side of sinful man?[1] God is met with a love equally holy—a love, therefore, no rendered by sinful man, but by a function of His own love in man; and rendered not by way of compromising the case by some pact, judicial or ritual; but so that the Holy Father comes to rest with infinite moral complacency in the personal achievement of the Holy Son, evermore saying, "This is My beloved Son, in whom I am well pleased." Father and Son dwell in each other in mutual personal satisfaction, full and joyful, evermore delighting in each other, and saying each to the other, "Holy, Holy, Holy, Heaven and earth are full of Thy glory."

Surely we have the same Christian call to rescue words like "satisfaction" from their popular travesties as the Apostles had (with an inspired insight) to save the divine idea of sacrifice and blood for its true, prime, and universal significance from its mere tribal *provenance*, and for a moral atonement from the mere ceremonialism of the day.

[1] The holiness of God is God as holy, just as "the decrees of God are God decreeing."

THE END.

Authors in the Biblical Classics Library:

C.K. Barrett
The Signs of an Apostle (19)
F.F. Bruce
Men and Movements in the Primitive Church (13)
The Message of the New Testament (1)
The Pauline Circle (14)
David Burnett
The Healing of the Nations (18)
Nigel Cameron
Complete in Christ (29)
D.A. Carson
From Triumphalism to Maturity (20)
Jesus and His Friends (15)
The Sermon on the Mount (2)
When Jesus Confronts the World (16)
James Denny
The Death of Christ (30)
The Christian Doctrine of Reconciliation (35)
H.L. Ellison
Men Spake from God (9)
The Message of the Old Testament (3)
P.T. Forsyth
The Cruciality of the Cross (31)
The Soul of Prayer (36)
John Goldingay
God's Prophet, God's Servant (5)
Graeme Goldsworthy
Gospel and Kingdom (4)
Gospel and Wisdom (10)
The Gospel in Revelation (6)
J.H. Greenlee
Scribes, Scrolls and Scripture (17)

A.M. Hunter
  Introducing New Testament Theology (26)
R.T. Kendall
  Believing God (11)
  Does Jesus Care? (25)
  Jonah (12)
  Once Saved, Always Saved (28)
George Knight
  Law and Grace (34)
I. Howard Marshall
  The Work of Christ (7)
Leon Morris
  The Cross of Jesus (8)
Lesslie Newbigin
  Trinitarian Doctrine for Today's Church (33)
J.N. Schofield
  Introducing Old Testament Theology (27)
Thomas Smail
  The Forgotten Father (23)
Helmut Thielicke
  A Little Exercise for Young Theologians (24)
Derek Tidball
  The Social Context of the New Testament (32)
John Wenham
  Easter Enigma (22)
A.M. Wolters
  Creation Regained (21)